Families would be enriched both spiritually and humanly if they read and applied the wisdom of St. Benedict as distilled by the author. *The Busy Family's Guide to Spirituality* is a rich book with many spiritual nuggets for the reader to mine and profit from.

— **John O'Connell,** Editor, *The Catholic Faith Magazine*

This book is a long-awaited gift for today's Christian family. For those families who are seeking more out of life, trying to incorporate deeply held Christian beliefs into the sometimes chaotic experience of family, or seeking ways to pray better and get along better, this book is ideal.

—*Spiritual Book News*

Many thanks for the gift of *The Busy Family's Guide to Spirituality*. I've shared the book with friends and all have gotten a little closer to God because of it.

— **Brother Martin,** monk, Our Lady of Guadalupe Trappist Abbey, Lafayette, Oregon

What sets *The Busy Family's Guide to Spirituality* apart from a whole library of parenting books is Robinson's use of the Rule of St. Benedict for each subtopic. Thus his family lessons are framed by the quietness and simplicity of the monastic way of life, while the tone of the book becomes one of contemplation rather than of family therapy or counseling.

— **Rhonda Beachy**

Families are a kind of monastic community. *The Busy Family's Guide to Spirituality* is a truly fresh and new resource for all who want their homes and families to be places of nurturing and safety and hope. This is practical and real and hope-filled, a must for every family — of every configuration.

— **Laura Swan, O.S.B.,** author of *Engaging Benedict: What the Rule Can Teach Us Today*

What a fresh perspective on family life! Having read a number of books about family life and raising children in a messed up world, this book has given my wife and me a new look at being a family. Combining the tradition of the Benedictine order and his own experience, David Robinson challenges the hectic lifestyle that so many families are caught up in today. It suggests a framework within which to truly be a family. Habits shape our lives. And this great book suggests that we create wonderful habits to shape our family life.

— **Steen Hudson,** father of three teenage sons

Robinson's enjoyable and easy-to-read prose made Benedict's rule come alive for me: I could easily see how to apply the rule to my family cloister.

— **John Davis,** dad, middle school teacher,
Oblate with St. Andrew Abbey

The Busy Family's Guide to Spirituality is packed with creative, practical ideas that Robinson has devised for deepening family spirituality and harmony. He gives us guidelines for establishing family meetings, lists of Scripture themes, simple ways to pray the psalms, and ideas for celebrating the liturgical seasons together. At the end of each chapter, family exercises offer practical activities for simple reference. *The Busy Family's Guide to Spirituality* is the most innovative book I have seen in the area of family spirituality. Like Benedict's Rule, *The Busy Family's Guide to Spirituality* is well grounded in Scripture. Benedict's spirituality lends itself to finding God in the everyday family environment, yet challenges us to seek greater holiness.

— *Spiritual Life: A Journal of
Contemporary Spirituality*

The Busy Family's
GUIDE TO SPIRITUALITY

The Busy Family's
GUIDE TO SPIRITUALITY

Practical Lessons for Modern Living from the Monastic Tradition

DAVID ROBINSON

A Crossroad Book
The Crossroad Publishing Company
New York

The Crossroad Publishing Company
www.CrossroadPublishing.com.

© 2009 by David Robinson

This book is a revised and updated version of an earlier Crossroad book, *The Family Cloister: Benedictine Wisdom for the Home,* © 2000 by David Robinson.

Unless otherwise noted, Scripture citations are from the Holy Bible, New International Version. Copyright © 1973, 1978, 1984 by International Bible Society. Used by permission of Zondervan Publishing House. All rights reserved.

Citations from *The Rule of St. Benedict* are used with the permission of Liturgical Press, Collegeville, Minn. The citations have been modified here in the interests of inclusive language. Some exercises in this book are adapted from *The Christian Family Toolbox: 52 Benedictine Activities for the Home* (New York: Crossroad Publishing Company, 2001), by David Robinson, and are used with the permission of The Crossroad Publishing Company, New York.

In continuation of our 200-year tradition of independent publishing, The Crossroad Publishing Company proudly offers a variety of books with strong, original voices and diverse perspectives. The viewpoints expressed in our books are not necessarily those of The Crossroad Publishing Company, any of its imprints, or of its employees. No claims are made or responsibility assumed for any health or other benefit.

Printed in the United States of America.

The text of this book is set in 12/15 Apollo.
The display face is Helvetica.

Library of Congress Cataloging-in-Publication Data

Robinson, David.
    The busy family's guide to spirituality: practical lessons for modern living from the monastic tradition / by David Robinson.
        p. cm.
    ISBN 10: 0-8245-2524-8
    ISBN 13: 978-0-8245-2524-8
    1. Family – Religious life Meditations. 2. Benedict, Saint, Abbot of Monte Cassino. Regula. I. Title.
    BV4526.2.R62 2000
    248.4 – dc21   99-16156

1   2   3   4   5   6   7   8   9   10   14   13   12   11   10   09

Stand at the crossroads and look;
ask for the ancient paths,
ask where the good way is, and walk in it,
and you will find rest for your souls.
— Jeremiah 6:16 —

Contents

Preface

You will be like a well-watered garden, like a spring whose waters never fail. —Isaiah 58:11

Several years ago, while hiking in the high country of Olympic National Park, our family came upon a spring of water bubbling boldly out of the ground a mile high along a ridgeline. That single spring watered a whole mountainside with the abundance of fresh water, helping to create a valley of stunning beauty. The water we gathered from this spring carried us further up along in our journey as a family. This collection of writings on family spirituality was inspired by an ancient spring, a guidebook for monastic families titled *The Rule of St. Benedict,* written in the early sixth century by Benedict of Nursia (ca. 480–ca. 547). Benedict's guidebook has guided communities of monks and nuns in their daily life for fifteen centuries. I've written this book for busy parents seeking a way to practice family spirituality with children in the home. Parents come in many shapes today. I've written for married parents, single parents, step-parents, non-custodial parents, bi-cultural parents, adoptive parents, and grandparents raising grandchildren. The principles and practices of

Benedictine spirituality may be applied to all such settings of family life.

Our family has changed in the past decade since *The Family Cloister* was first published in 2000 (Note: the title, *The Family Cloister* was changed to *The Busy Family's Guide to Spirituality* for this revised, updated edition.) In 2005, our youngest son went off to college, leaving us with an empty nest for much of the year. Two of our sons have married, bringing us the gift of two beautiful daughters-in-love. We still live in the coastal village of Cannon Beach on the north Oregon coast. I have served as pastor of Community Presbyterian Church in Cannon Beach, Oregon since 1993. This family of faith has taught me the meaning of true loving community through their hospitality and service to others.

Since this book was first published, many types of groups, including study groups, book clubs, home-schooling support groups, parent-teacher organizations, and church parenting groups have studied this book and discovered wisdom helpful in guiding their families into a spiritual way of living. My hope as you read this book is that you will find encouragement in your spiritual parenting as you seek to raise your children in the way of faith, hope and love.

The Busy Family's Guide to Spirituality follows the pattern laid out in *The Rule of St. Benedict.* [1] For this edition, I've added a section of practical exercises at the end of each chapter with lessons drawn from monastic life to support you in your family life together. Like a natural spring that wells up and overflows, the ancient wisdom

of St. Benedict continues to offer refreshment to those
who journey together into family spirituality. Through
all the changes, across many generations, the pure water
from Benedict's wisdom pours forth with refreshment
as much today as it did fifteen hundred years ago when
the monks of Monte Cassino first drew water from the
spring of Benedict's *Rule*. My hope for you and your
family is that you will find spiritual refreshment and
wisdom for raising your children with joy as you draw
water from the ancient spring of family spirituality.

David Robinson
Cannon Beach, Oregon
May 2009

Introduction

Strength to the Body and Soul

Everybody needs beauty as well as bread, places to play in and pray in where nature may heal and cheer and give strength to the body and soul.
— John Muir

Every year, just before we set out on our annual week-long family hiking adventure, we gather together at the trailhead, hold hands in a circle, and pray for God's presence to be with us in our journey ahead. This simple act of devotion is the essence of family spirituality. Fifteen hundred years ago, Benedict gathered a family of monks around a common life of prayer and work. The insights he learned over several decades of life together with his family, he wrote down in a practical, spiritual guidebook, *The Rule of St. Benedict*. I believe Benedict has wisdom and guidance to offer the 21st-century family. As your family begins to practice this way of spiritual life together, you will discover you've set out together upon a new path, a wonderful journey to a fulfilled family life. Like *The Rule of St. Benedict*, this book is *written for beginners* (RB, 73), for busy parents who may be looking for support and encouragement in the adventure of raising children.[2]

Since October 1986, I've enjoyed annual monastic retreats at Benedictine abbeys in Oregon, California, New Mexico, Kentucky, and Georgia. While on these retreats, I've often thought about *The Rule of St. Benedict,* which was written in a time of great societal change. Cities were being overthrown and political powers were in turmoil. Instability, violence, corruption, disease, and hunger were the common enemies of Benedict's day. Under the guidance of the *Rule,* within the protective walls of the abbey, monastic communities became havens of stability in medieval society. Many of the basic building blocks of Western civilization such as libraries and schools, books and literacy, medicine and the arts, agriculture and industry, even the practice of charity and hospitality, owe a great debt to the widespread influence of Benedict and his *Rule.*

Fifteen hundred years later, thousands of monastic communities around the world still live according to the wisdom of Benedict in their daily lives, praying, studying, and working together as a monastic family under the direction of the *Rule.* Modern monastic communities have made their own adaptations and revisions of Benedict's *Rule,* something I offer here on behalf of families today.

As parents, we step into family life with very little training. We are handed some gear and equipment in the form of advice and experience from our parents and grandparents. We are offered a few tools by people around us. Then we step out into the adventure of family life. Life in the family has been both harder and more delightful than I imagined three decades ago. Every day has been filled with more than enough lists, demands, and interruptions. Parents are busy people. The practical work of parenting sometimes overwhelms the joy of raising children. Just as soon as we begin to figure it out, our kids grow out of one phase and enter a whole new one. The adventure of parenting continues as we learn new roles in each unfamiliar part of the journey of family life.

Two simple prayers come to mind for the journey: Thanks! and Help! Before our children graduated from diapers, they had learned these prayers. Night by night, we prayed together at bedtime offering God a combination of these two basic prayers. After our children were asleep, we'd enter their rooms and pray our own prayers of thanks and help. Thanks, God, for sharing with us the gift of raising these beautiful children. Dear God, help us raise our children in your good way. Somewhere between our prayers of thanks and cries for help, we've asked each other many questions about this spiritual calling of parenting. Where is there time for developing the spiritual lives of our children? How do faith, hope, and love fit into the family portrait? As a busy family, how can we keep from wearing out? Family life can get so rushed and disjointed that there seems little time left for God. The way into family spirituality remains hidden for many families.

What is family spirituality? Imagine something like a beautiful, well-watered garden. Mary Lennox in Francis

Hodgson Burnett's classic children's tale, *The Secret Garden,* discovered the door into her secret garden with the help of the robin. Likewise, we may need help finding the way into family spirituality. Burnett writes a lovely description of Mary's first experience within an English walled garden:

> She took another long breath, because she could not help it, and she held back the swinging curtain of ivy and pushed back the door which opened slowly — slowly. Then she slipped through it, and shut it behind her, and stood with her back against it, looking about her and breathing quite fast with excitement, and wonder, and delight. She was standing inside the secret garden. It was the sweetest, most mysterious-looking place anyone could imagine. The high walls which shut it in were covered with the leafless stems of climbing roses which were so thick that they were matted together. . . . She moved away from the door, stepping as softly as if she were afraid of awakening someone. She was glad that there was grass under her feet and that her steps made no sounds.[3]

Those first few steps through the doorway into the garden of family spirituality lead us into a delightful new world, "the sweetest, most mysterious-looking place anyone could imagine." As you enter together with your children, take beginning steps along the pathway before you. At first, these steps may seem strange. When we quiet our hearts and listen, we will hear a call from long ago, inviting us into an adventure, into a whole new way of living. "Ask for the ancient paths, ask where the good way is, and walk in it, and you will find rest for your souls."[4]

How can busy families find their way into spiritual life together? Benedict offers us several beginning steps of faith, including prayer, study, and love. *First of all, every time you begin a good work, you must pray to God most earnestly to bring it to perfection* (RB, Prologue). As Benedict reveals in the *Rule,* our first step of faith is to begin with prayer, entering into conversation with God as friend and guide. We take a second step into family spirituality when we study God's guidebook, the Scriptures. Through regular time in study, the light of God's wisdom begins to fill our mind and the voice of God's love fills our heart. Life with God is not only about words, but also about deeds. A third beginning step into family spirituality involves putting love into action in the places where we live and work. As we practice a life of love in action over months and years, we will grow together as a family in unexpected ways.

Such growth doesn't come instantly or quickly. Many times since we began our family journey together in 1981, we've packed our backpacks and stepped out as a family at a trailhead, taking the first steps of a new journey into a beautiful forest of tall trees. We've hiked as a family along moss-lined paths through stands of old-growth timber, an experience something like walking in a natural cathedral. Like a growing forest, family spirituality does not spring up overnight. Though there will always be laundry and dishes to be cleaned, we need not be in a hurry within the family. Love and wisdom emerge in family life like fir saplings springing up from the good earth. To change from selfish ways to spiritual ways requires time and patience along with God's help.

There are other ways to live as a family, including dead-end alleyways, busy ways full of lists and demands, selfish ways leading to boredom, and freeways carrying us nowhere fast. According to Benedict, the good way for the family lies beyond the secret gate, within the creative and loving embrace of family spirituality. Benedict offers families a wealth of wisdom, even across fifteen centuries of time. As we listen and put into practice the wisdom of Benedict, we will be strengthened in our love for God and for one another.

Though we make a good start, we easily grow weary and fail in our efforts to love one another. As a father, I live too often in the shadow of regret, fear, and weariness and not enough in the light of gratitude, faith, and love. A slogan that often describes my life is, "Why pray when I can worry." To walk by faith does not imply we are perfect. As parents, we need encouragement every day in the challenge of raising healthy, loving children. I believe parents possess all the gifts necessary to raise children in the life of love.

In the pages ahead I hope to reflect with you upon family life in the light of Benedict's *Rule*. I follow the *Rule* chapter by chapter through this book, drawing upon ancient wisdom, applying Benedict's insights to family life today. For you, family life may involve a two-parent family, a single-parent family, a mixed faith marriage, a multi-cultural family, a blended family with step-children, grandparents raising grandchildren or adoptive family members. The ancient principles found in these pages apply to each of these unique family situations, offering a space where children and adults share in life together with God in their midst. This book also offers guidance and encouragement for people who work with families, such as teachers, parish professionals, priests, pastors, educators, social workers and child-care providers.

At the end of each chapter, you'll find a variety of exercises, including family activities, surveys, resources and discussion questions for strengthening the body and soul of your family life together.

If this book encourages you in your spiritual calling as a parent, I've accomplished what I set out to write. I believe God's desire for the family is that we live a life of love, as we journey together on paths into family spirituality. Ever rooted in God's wisdom, ever growing in God's love, we shall, as Benedict writes, *progress in this way of life and in faith, our hearts overflowing with the inexpressible delight of love* (RB, Prologue).

Chapter One

Create Your Home

Choosing a Proven Blueprint for Your Life

Everyone who hears these words of mine and puts them into practice is like a wise man who built his house on the rock. — Matthew 7:24

I vividly recall my first visit to a monastery in October 1986, and the deep sense of peace which came upon me as I sat quietly in the cloister garden. I had come home. Monasteries offer a beautiful design that serves the needs and purposes of the monastic community as well as those who come as guests. You'll almost always find an enclosed garden at the center of the monastery, surrounded by the sanctuary, dining hall, kitchen, and dormitory. Nearby, you'll find the guest house along with other rooms including workshops, an infirmary, and the library.

Like the design of a monastery, blueprints for family spirituality are designed to serve the needs and purposes of families seeking to live together in love. My wife and I shared many conversations regarding patterns of parenting when we became pregnant with our firstborn. Choosing a family blueprint is not easy, but it is essential for the crafting of a well-built family. Benedict's design for communal spiritual life has stood the test of time, and can offer busy families today wisdom and guidance for finding their way home.

Benedict's family was a community of monks, living under the leadership of an abbot or "father," and guided by a common "rule of life." The word "rule," used throughout, comes from the Latin word *regula,* meaning a measuring tool or guidebook. From the foundation of Benedict's *Rule,* written in the sixth century, there developed thousands of long-enduring spiritual communities across the landscape of Europe, and later around the world, providing stability and wisdom across generations.

Every family lives according to some type of design whether consciously or not. But without a wise blueprint and a good foundation, a family may not endure the storms that lie ahead. Many parents I know have combined family blueprints from their upbringings. Most parents also seek guidance in the ongoing challenge of raising children. In this chapter we will survey a variety of blueprints for family spirituality, and then look at patterns for family life within those structures.

Basic Family Designs

Your current family life may not represent the home you envisioned when you first thought about starting a family and raising children. Often, parents feel trapped in a pattern of family life they didn't choose. Drawing inspiration from the *Rule,* I want to briefly explore a few basic family blueprints in our time: the *life-apart* family, the *life-without-rules* family, the *life-on-the-move* family, and the *life-together* family. No matter what pattern you find in your home today, I believe change is possible when new family designs are put into practice.

The Life-Apart Family

Talk with most parents today and they will tell you they are very busy. Parents have a hard time getting everyone together in the same room at the same time. There are many demands that pull the family apart, isolating family members in separate worlds. These "worlds" may include busy schedules, careers, business travels, electronic media, school events, and other extracurricular activities. Separation is a normal part of family life in healthy families. Every parent needs time away without interruptions: to soak in a hot bath, to go for a walk, or just to sit and pay the bills. Every child needs time alone to play and dream. One of the creative challenges in family life is finding a healthy balance between individuality and community. Many families today overemphasize the individual at the expense of the family community, and thus live in isolation from one another, though they may live under the same roof. Another form of the *life-apart family* is divorce. Though children are very resilient and adjust to living between two homes, the impact of a divorce can be felt by the family years later. Parents who have gone through divorce often discover renewed strength and support to raise their children. What a joy to see careful renovation in family construction, when *life-apart* parents begin to discover ways to rebuild their family according to a new design.

The Life-Without-Rules Family

Another possible blueprint for families is the *life-without-rules* family. Busy families sometimes give up on any regular structure or intentional shared life in the home. A common cultural attitude today rejects rules and regulations, replacing them instead with feelings and intuitions. Surrounded by such a culture, how can a family find guidance for raising children? What is the place of rules and structures in the home? How can parents find the creative balance between discipline and freedom? Such questions confront all parents who seek to navigate the challenging journey of raising children. Finding the balance between discipline and freedom is no easy task. Permissive families allow individual preferences and passions to replace the structure of shared family commitments. Legalistic families crush the human spirit with rigid rules and regulations. When this balance is lost, family foundations are subjected to erosion. Families that give up on structure in the home fail to provide children with security and stability, while overly disciplined families may leave little room for personal freedom and tenderness.

The Life-on-the-Move Family

Another common design for families today is a pattern I call *life-on-the-move*. Busy families today are often on the go, driving kids to multiple events each week, including sports practices, music lessons, games, clubs, meetings and other activities. Parents become the local taxi service for kids. When our kids were teens, we put up all our family schedules on a master calendar on the bulletin board in the kitchen just to make sure we knew where everyone needed to be on any given day. Within every family lies the creative tension between mobility and stability. We want our children to explore and have wonderful adventures out on their own. Yet, we also want them home, sharing life with the family well-rooted in love. Family spirituality does not spring up overnight. Our culture emphasizes fast ways of living: fast food, fast Internet service, instant gratification, and instant communication. This pace can lead to a feeling of instability and make it hard for families to put down strong spiritual roots. In our time, busy families often rush from place to place, unable to settle down for any length of time or share even a few meals together as a family. Family spiritual life grows slowly, taking root and maturing over years.

The Life-Together Family

As you review the family blueprints above, perhaps one of them describes your family life more than the others. If your family is anything like ours, you have inevitably experienced the push and pull of tensions upon your family life together. What is the *life-together* family? This way of family life involves sharing a life of love with God and with one another in our daily life as a family. I readily admit to being far from the

life-together ideal in our family. We've known all the
other three patterns of family life at different times in
our home. Speaking of those first three blueprints for
family life, Benedict writes *Let us pass them by, then,
and . . . proceed to draw up a plan for the strong kind*
(RB, 1). The "strong kind" of life Benedict refers to is
what I'm calling the "life together" family. Even the
strongest families face seductive powers that threaten to
pull the family apart. Even the healthiest families wrestle with the balance of freedom and responsibility. Even
the best-rooted families are tempted by opportunities
to pick up and move over the rainbow to some distant
Land of Oz. No matter which form of family life you
experience currently in your home, in the pages ahead
let us press on together to better understand Benedict's
blueprints for the *life-together* family.

Building Blocks for Parents

Our kids have always loved playing with Legos, spending hours upon hours building cities, cars and castles,
and filling these with their creative imaginations. In a
similar manner, young parents spend hours upon hours
putting into place the basic building blocks of family
life. We enter into parenting with plenty of imagination
and little experience. Parenting is on-the-job training
from day one. Along the way, we begin to learn basic
skills that we can use as building blocks for creating
a family. We pick up these building blocks from many
sources, including role models from our childhood.

Benedict envisioned the monastery as a family with definite roles of leadership to help guide the family into spiritual maturity. Leadership in the monastery has everything to do with setting a loving example that promotes spiritual growth in the community. What would promote such growth in your family? What core values or building blocks are available for parents today? Below we will survey five qualities of excellence, or "building blocks" for parents.

Genuine Encounter

In Benedict's view, the abbot represents the loving presence of God to the monastic family. In a similar fashion, as parents we seek to exemplify the loving presence of God to our children. One way we do this is by paying attention to our children through "genuine encounter" with them. Dorothy Corkille Briggs's book *Your Child's Self-Esteem* speaks effectively to this.

> Every child needs focused attention — genuine encounter — to feel loved. Your child is likely to view continual distancing — concern with the past, future, schedules, and tasks — as lack of love. He can only feel lovable if you take time to be fully with his person. Make a habit of being open to the wonder of your child in the here-and-now.[5]

My father seemed to intuitively understand this. One summer during my teenage years, my dad completely refinished and restored our old upright piano. That same year, dad built a full size, gull-wing sports car with my brother. He did this to enter into the world of his teenage sons. I was a beginning jazz pianist; my brother loved fast cars. Now, as a father with my own grown children, I look back and marvel at my dad's wisdom. In his mid-forties, he exemplified the presence of God by stepping out of his adult position of power in order to enter into the interests and passions of his kids. One of the greatest gifts we can give our children is our full attention. This is difficult for busy parents on the go. When our minds are full of schedules and demands, we leave little space for our children. We can enter our children's lives by getting down on their level, eye-to-eye, giving our full selves to them through active listening. This is not always easy, especially at the end of a tiring day of work. Sometimes my wife and I have foolishly figured that dishes, phone calls, and checkbooks take precedence over listening to our children. Five minutes a day of genuine encounter with our children can dramatically impact them for a lifetime. It is in our willingness to come down from our lofty heights as adults and truly enter the world of our children that they will discover God's love shining through our life.

Teach by Example

Instead of the familiar parenting proverb, "Do as I say, not as I do," it would be better to tell our children, "Live as I live and learn from my mistakes." As Benedict warns, *point out to [them] all that is good and holy more by example than by words* (RB, 2). We teach children more through our example than through our words. When we've fallen short in our life with our children,

we should attempt to set things right through exempli-
fying honesty. In my experience as a parent, exemplary
living does not come easily. Anger, pride, frustration,
tiredness, and depression are a few of the factors that
get in the way of this type of parenting. When I have
been too harsh with one of our boys, I know it inwardly.
There is a place in all parents where we feel a sense of
regret over our shortcomings. As parents we are wise to
go to our children and ask for forgiveness when we've
been overly harsh, unkind, or inconsistent. With God's
help, we are reunited and our relationship deepens. At
times it seems, not only are we raising children, our
children are raising us.

Care for the Soul

Children are gifts from God. They reflect in their lives
the quality of the care given them. As parents, we are
wise to care for our children's inner life. As Benedict
writes, *keep in mind that [we] have undertaken the care
of souls for whom [we] must give an account* (RB, 2).
Parenting involves the care of the souls, or nurturing
of our children's inner lives. Soul-care means tending
to the inner growth of our kids. Though they are with
us for a few decades, ultimately, our children belong to
God. When I look upon my children as belonging to me,
I get caught up too easily in my reputation, my needs,
and my irritation at their lack of maturity. When we
welcome our children as gifts from God, we live with
gratitude for who they are and find greater freedom to
nurture the life of their souls.

Show Equal Love

Benedict instructs us, *show equal love to everyone and apply the same discipline to all according to their merits* (RB, 2). These recommendations are tempered with the advice that *[We] must so accommodate and adapt [ourselves] to each one's character and intelligence* (RB, 2). The tension between these two directives can help us negotiate issues of favoritism in our families. Every member of the family is unique; we love each child uniquely. Different family members have different gifts and needs. Some are more sensitive of heart. Others are able to take the rough-and-tumble and come out unhurt. In the family, every member is treasured and offers something of worth. Thus, we seek to love every child uniquely, offering each member of the family training, support, and acceptance according to the need and situation. Benedict encourages us to tailor our approach to the individuality of the person: one may best be taught according to the heart, another through the mind, another by the body. Wise parents adapt their lessons to each individual child so no one is left out and all are cared for and guided in a way that suits them best.

Celebrate Growth

Look for signs of spiritual growth in your family. Every spring, we take time as a family to observe the buds and new shoots emerging from the good earth. In the same way, learn to celebrate the budding of spiritual life in your family. Today we step forward in the adventure of parenting. Take time daily to enjoy the adventure. As parents we are people of hope, looking forward to the wonders in store for their children around every bend in the road. As we see new life in our children, we can rejoice and give thanks to God. As grandparents, we'll look back and think of all the wonders we shared with our kids: learning to play jazz piano, cruising the loop in a homemade sports car or getting on our hands and knees with our grandchildren to play Legos once again.

Family Meetings

Another common design of the *life-together family* involves regular family meetings. As I've traveled around the nation I've often asked parents how often their families meet together. Most families seldom meet for family meetings. Many do not meet at all. In contrast, monks meet together weekly in "the chapter room" to read a chapter of the *Rule* and discuss family issues together. As Benedict writes: *As often as anything important is to be done in the monastery, the abbot shall call the whole community together* (RB, 3). All the chapter rooms I've ever visited have been lined with wooden benches, apparently to discourage nodding off during family meetings. Monks know that life together is always a work in progress.

Commitment to Meet as a Family

In our family life over the past two decades, we've gathered regularly for family meetings. Holding family meetings grew increasingly difficult with all our competing schedules, and sometimes we went several weeks or even months without a family meeting. Though we've often skipped family meetings due to our schedules, we've been committed to meet together as a family and have enjoyed many great family meetings over the years.

Encouragement

At our family meetings, we take time for encouragement, discussion, games, and prayer. We begin with encouragement. Our family meetings often start with sharing stories about our week while eating dessert together. We encourage each person to say something encouraging about another family member. Praise and encouragement gets a family meeting going in a positive direction from the beginning.

Discussion

Next, we discuss specific issues facing the family. Every family member is encouraged to express views and ideas in family counsel, whatever their age. As Benedict instructs: *The reason why we have said all should be called for counsel is that the Spirit often reveals what is better to the younger* (RB, 3). We also take time to listen to the views and voices of other family members. Parents are like gardeners. We plant seeds, care for seedlings, and pull weeds, but it is God who brings the growth. Having heard the voice of the family on certain issues, parents guide the family to make decisions. We record the decisions in a family journal.

Games

Besides discussing family issues, we love to play games together. Sometimes we'll throw a surprise into the middle of a family meeting: make-your-own-banana-split, beach bonfire night, and tickle tag-team wrestling are a few activities that have memorably livened up this time together. Creativity, laughter, and playfulness are the fizz and bubble in family meetings that keep our children coming back for more.

Prayer

At the close of a family meeting, we like to light a candle, hold hands in a circle and offer our thanks to God. Maybe you do not currently have times of family prayer in your home. Consider adding a moment of silence at the end of your family meeting to allow everyone to offer a quiet gift of thanks. We've enjoyed uniting our voices and spirits in gratitude to God at the end of family meetings.

Other Approaches

Family meetings come in many shapes and sizes. If the idea of gathering your whole family together in one room to discuss family issues seems too daunting a task, try meeting one-on-one, parent to child. Another approach may be talking about family matters right after dinner once a week at the dinner table. Occasional family meetings are preferable to never meeting as a family. The goal is sharing life together and working to create a home where everyone can truly love and grow.

At first, your family may find it helpful to keep family meetings on the short side, under thirty minutes, with more encouragement and play, and less family business and problem solving. As this habit develops and family members learn the importance of this family blueprint, the length may be expanded to meet greater needs among family members. For more specific ideas for holding a family meeting, see the *Exercises* section at the end of this chapter.

Family Construction Tools

Like most homes, over the years we've accumulated a wide variety of tools to help with various family projects and chores around the house. Every week, these tools step forward to assist our family. Mr. and Mrs. Kenmore work side-by-side in our laundry room, faithfully cleaning our clothes. Miele never seems to tire of picking up the dirt from our carpets, while young Bosch quietly washes the dishes. Families, like homes, require certain tools and excellence in craftsmanship.

Benedict understood that the spiritual life required careful craftsmanship. The motto often associated with Benedictines is "pray and work."[6] Benedict believed the real work of a monk was the work of prayer. Benedict also believed in the value of manual labor for monks. Thus, every Benedictine monastery includes workshops and prayer chapels where monks work together with body and spirit to support the community and care for the world around. So it should not come as a surprise to read in the *Rule* when Benedict lists seventy-three tools of the trade for the labor of building a spiritual family. As parents we are wise to acquire spiritual tools of love and learn to use them in our home as though in a craftsman's workshop. As Benedict writes, *the workshop where we are to toil faithfully at all these tasks is the enclosure . . . and stability in the community* (RB, 4).

At the end of this chapter, in the *Exercises* section, I've adapted Benedict's list of tools for good works, gathering them into months. Perhaps you will find it helpful to employ these various tools in your family by trying them out for a period of time. Check in with family members during that time to discover how they are putting these tools into use in their lives. *These, then, are the tools of the spiritual craft* (RB, 4), writes Benedict, understanding the monastic family as a workshop where God's spiritual craftsmanship is at work. In a similar manner, the family grows year after year as family members learn to use the tools of love. By these, your family will be shaped more and more into a well-crafted home. At family meetings, you may want to discuss practical ways to put these tools to work in your home and community. As you implement these family tools of love, you'll see spiritual craftsmanship at work in your home.

Like home builders, we consult our family blueprints, and working together we craft our home into a place of excellence, beauty, and love. In our family, even when the dirty laundry piled up and chores were neglected, we've still seen God's goodness at work in our lives through these tools of love. The final spiritual tool on Benedict's list is hope, the quiet confidence that the blueprint of our family is being built before our very eyes. *Finally, never lose hope in God's mercy* (RB, 4).

Follow the Leader

It wasn't until I was an adult rafting down the Ocoee River in Tennessee that I realized the life importance of the childhood game "follow the leader." Our whitewater guide taught us three commands: paddle forward, paddle backward, and drift. He assured us no one would drown if we followed his commands. As we launched our seven-person raft into the first set of rapids called Snow White and the Seven Dwarfs, our guide soberly informed us that someone had drowned the previous week riding alone on an inner-tube through those same rapids. "This river is not a nice lady," he called out over the roar of the white water, "so follow my commands!" We listened to our guide's commands, followed the leader, and made it down the wild Ocoee River, thanks to the wisdom of an experienced guide.

When we welcome spirituality into our family life, we enter into something like the game of "follow the leader" as a family. Together, we learn to listen to God's guidance and put into practice God's instructions. As a kind of river guide, God helps to direct our lives through the rapids and we begin to live life more fully. Try to journey alone and we open our lives to a wide array of dangers. One of the basic blueprints for spiritual parenting is learning to "follow the leader," or learning to accept the guidance of others.

Obedience in the family simply means that the guidance of another becomes more important than my own individual will. In the monastery, along with fidelity and stability, obedience stands as one of three basic commitments monks take for life. In Benedict's words, *They no longer live by their own judgment, giving in to their whims and appetites; rather they walk according to another's decision and directions* (RB, 5). Benedict taught that following the leader was necessary for spiritual maturity. He describes this way of living as being motivated by love. *It is love that impels them to pursue everlasting life; therefore, they are eager to take the narrow road* (RB, 5).

Naturally, the human spirit can be resistant to following any leader. Following a leader lacks the adrenaline and glory of being driven by will alone. Obedience is not a sprint but a life-long journey. Many obstacles to following a leader can crop up: fear, arrogance, and laziness, to name a few. Such obstacles in family life may cause much anguish and suffering and keep us from enjoying the fullness that God intends for us. When children wander away from the path of wisdom and goodness, spiritual parents keep calling their children back, helping them into a life of "following the leader." I believe we do this best by offering ourselves as examples. We listen to and act on God's guidance to the best of our ability. Like the river guide on the Ocoee, we only have a few commands to follow: love God, love each other, and rest in God's love. We cheer our children on as they carry out these basic commands, seeking to show them the adventurous way of love through our own lives. I believe when we travel this way together, our children will catch on, learn to listen to the river guide, and discover the delight of following the leader.

The Gift of Silence

Family life can be very noisy. Raising children also means raising the decibel level in our homes. Every six months or so, my word-weary spirit begins to call to me, inviting me to come back to the quiet. I accept the gift of silence by getting away to a monastery for several days. This doesn't come naturally or easily. But after a few days of soaking my life in the silence of the abbey, God's healing work begins to take effect, preparing me to enter once again into the world of words. Bringing this gift of silence into our families rejuvenates and refreshes our lives together.

Certain forms of speech do not belong in the family. We've refused to allow deceitful talk, disrespectful talk, or trash talk in our home. I can still hear my parents telling me, "If you can't say something nice, don't say anything at all." The Bible offers similar instruction: "When words are many, sin is not absent, but he who holds his tongue is wise."[7] This proverb is just as true for parents as it is for children. One of the most powerful ways to remove garbage speech from the home is to welcome the gift of silence. Through daily times of quiet in the home we invite our children into deepening life with God. If we cannot speak of what is good, beautiful, and true, we will likely waste our words.

Benedict highly valued silence in the monastic family. *There are times when good words are to be left unsaid out of esteem for silence. Indeed, so important is silence that permission to speak should seldom be granted even to mature disciples, no matter how good or holy or constructive their talk* (RB, 6).

Benedict lived in a very busy world. Like homes today, monasteries could easily have become bustling places full of words and non-stop activity. Though monks are not against human conversation, they esteem silence as a gift to be treasured. Every time I return to the abbey, I'm awed by the enfolding sense of silence. More than merely the cessation of human speech, silence is like a deep well full of cool water. All who come to this well find refreshment. Out of this deep well of silence, God spoke creation into being. Out of the gift of silence in our homes, God's creative voice continues to bring forth life and goodness to our family.

Not all silence in the family is a gift. Silence can be used as a weapon, a shield from injury, or a cover-up for spiritual sickness. Some use silence to inflict pain upon others, refusing to speak or withholding vulnerability and intimacy. Others have been hurt with words and withdraw into silence to protect themselves from further pain. Still others hide behind silence, outwardly pretending that all is well when inwardly they are dying for connection and love. When we bring our lives into God's quiet presence, God quenches our inner thirst for love and invites us to enter once again into the gift of healthy silence. From this gift emerges the wisdom in the best use of speech.

One of the most difficult design aspects to visualize in a house plan is open space, the open area of a room, wall-to-wall, floor-to-ceiling. Most of the interior of a well-built home is simply open space. Likewise, most of the space within the family is filled with silence. Among busy families, the gift of silence may be hard to imagine, let alone enjoy. As we enter into family spirituality, we open ourselves to the wonder of sacred silence and begin to listen to the quiet voice of God in our lives.

Twelve Small Steps

The entryway into family spirituality is constructed of twelve small steps. Those who walk up these steps discover more of the beautiful design for the *life-together* family. Benedict calls these stairs the "steps of humility." As parents, we try to take these small steps and also teach them to our children. Here's a brief look at Benedict's twelve small steps of humility and how they may help our families.

1. Focus

Benedict instructs us to get our eyes off self and onto God: *The first step of humility, then, is that we keep "the reverence of God always before our eyes" (Psalm 36:2) and never forget it* (RB, 7). What we focus on is what we become, when we focus upon the beauty and goodness of God and we allow our inner lives to be filled with beauty and goodness. We are wise to look to God first thing in the morning, even before we look at our own faces in the mirror. Ask God for help in focusing your eyes on goodness, truth, and love through the day.

2. Imitate

The second step of humility is that we love not our own will nor take pleasure in the satisfaction of our desires; rather we shall imitate by our actions that saying of Christ's: "I have come not to do my own will, but the will of the One who sent me" (John 6:38; RB, 7). Our own will is ever before us, demanding attention. Within family spirituality, God quietly steps in, offering guidance and motivation for our actions. Do I seek to follow God's guidance more than my own? When we cherish God's guidance above our own, we will more eagerly seek to imitate God's way of love in our lives day by day. The second small step is to imitate "by our actions" the life and ways of God.

3. Respect

At the end of each day in the monastery, every monk bows before the abbot to receive a night blessing. This quiet act is a living example of Benedict's third small step of humility, *that we submit to [others] in all obedience for the love of God* (RB, 7). Respect for older and wiser people is at the heart of the spiritual life. To lay down my life for my family is to love my family by respecting each member of my family. Every member in the family is asked to live with respect, including parents and children. In our hearts, we respect each person in our family as though they were someone worthy of a bow at the end of the day.

4. Persevere

In Benedict's words, *The fourth step of humility is that in this obedience under difficult, unfavorable, or even unjust conditions, our hearts quietly embrace suffering and endure it without weakening or seeking escape* (RB, 7). We usually do not choose the hassles or pains we face. They just come along. One of the challenges of healthy family life lies in how we face our afflictions. The third small step asks us to live without much whining or complaining. In the face of unlooked-for suffering, we ask for strength and patience to endure difficulties without making a big fuss. Just as the flow of water gets diverted through corroded pipes in a house, family goodness leaks out through grumbling, leaving the family dry and thirsty for love. Through the habit of perseverance, these leaky pipes are repaired and members of the family find their lives renewed.

5. Wash

Through our selfish ways, greed, or thoughtlessness, we pile up mounds of dirty laundry around our lives. Any family knows what happens when the laundry is neglected for several weeks. We begin running out of clean underwear and socks. Then the complaining begins. Basic to the health of the busy family is the habit of admitting mistakes and forgiving each other. As we find in the Rule, *The fifth step of humility is that we do not conceal from the abbot any sinful thoughts entering our hearts, or any wrongs committed in secret, but rather confess them humbly* (RB, 7). Basic to family spiritual

health is washing up regularly, that is, honestly admitting our shortcomings and seeking the cleansing gift of forgiveness.

6. Be Content

The sixth step of humility is that we are content with the lowest and most menial treatment (RB, 7). A core truth in family spirituality is that people matter more than things. Contentment is a counterforce to consumer appetites of greed and excessive accumulation. A life of contentment arises from a resting heart that has ceased striving after excess, but instead has begun to find pleasure in natural gifts such as rain and laughter. Like monastic families, we too can learn to live simply with contentment. A good resource book, offering many excellent ideas for simple family living, is Elaine St. James' *Simplify Your Life: 100 Ways to Make Family Life Easier and More Fun.* [8]

7. Accept

The seventh step of humility is that we not only admit with our tongues but are also convinced in our hearts that we are inferior to all (RB, 7). Benedict was not afflicted with an inferiority complex, nor did he desire such of his brothers. Instead, he taught a life habit of simply accepting our place in the universe. I live in a rural place without many city lights to block out starlight. When I look up at the stars, a twin sense of grandeur and humility comes over my spirit. Acceptance is quietly discovering who we are in this grand universe. We are not the center. Our lives are brief. Our strength is limited. We are finite. Yet, we are loved. To accept our limitations while marveling at the greatness of God's love prepares us to live more completely and lovingly within the family.

8. Yield

The eighth step of humility is marked by a yellow triangle pointing downward. As Benedict puts it: *The eighth step of humility is that we do only what is endorsed by the common rule of the monastery and the example set by the abbot* (RB, 7). A healthy family learns how to yield to one another. Even as we step together through a doorway, one person usually yields to the other to allow a smooth entry. The small step of yielding to let another have the way is basic to the design of family spirituality. Every day, opportunities arise to practice yielding to one another. From this small step emerges a spirit of goodwill and cooperation in the family.

9. Listen

The ninth step of humility is that we control our tongues (RB, 7). On the north end of our town is the mouth of Ecola Creek where it flows into the ocean. The tides come and go up this mouth, filling the creek with a brackish mixture of fresh and salt water. Our mouths can easily fill up with a strange mix of fresh water and salt water. "Out of the same mouth come praise and cursing. My brothers, this should not be. Can both fresh water and salt water flow from the same spring?"[9] When we give open flow to our words, they easily get mixed up with our pride, lust, and greed. When we allow our hearts to listen, our lives are filled with freshness. Healthy families learn to listen to one another, and thus use words to build others up in love.

10. Build Up

Benedict warns us in the tenth step of humility against the careless use of laughter in the family. Closely related to the previous step, this step refines the use of words within the family. Each family member learns to use words that will build up others. Often, with family members who are weary or self-centered, words come tumbling out that are sharp, hurtful, or empty. These words may be spoken in a joking manner to soften the blow or make the impact seem like it was "just a joke." As parents, we are wise to encourage the use of words that will edify members of the family.

11. Speak Gently

The eleventh step of humility is that we speak gently . . . and with becoming modesty, briefly and reasonably, but without raising our voices (RB, 7). In this step Benedict calls the community to gentleness in our use of words. Learning to speak honestly and lovingly is one of the most important skills for a rich life. We err easily on one side or another of this narrow road of speech. Some will blurt out whatever they may be feeling at the time, speaking the truth without any consideration of the impact of their words. Others hide their feelings, afraid to come out with inner problems for fear of being rejected. When we learn to speak gently, we grow up into the full maturity of love.

12. Love

The twelfth and final small step is the invitation to live a life of love in our daily experience. Benedict phrases it this way: *The twelfth step of humility is that we always manifest humility in our bearing no less than in our hearts* (RB, 7). As we put these twelve small steps into action in our hearts, love becomes a way of life within the home. A life of humility is more than mere words or actions. We live this way of life in our outward appearances as in our actions, in our thoughts as in our hearts, with others as when alone. "It is easy to love the people far away," wrote Mother Teresa of Calcutta. "It is not always easy to love those close to us. It is easier to give a cup of rice to relieve hunger than to relieve the loneliness and pain of someone unloved in our own home. Bring love into your home, for this is where our love for each other must start."[10]

As parents, we set an example for the whole family through our daily attitudes by bringing love into our home. While the world around us seeks to climb and grasp at ever-greater heights of fortune and glory, the family quietly steps into family spirituality. Children will catch on to this new way of living, especially when given an example to follow. Though "it is not always easy to love those close to us," by walking along these twelve small steps and putting into practice some of the blueprints laid out in this chapter, we will discover a greater capacity to love one another and "relieve the loneliness and pain" of unloved people in our family, community, and world.

FAMILY BLUEPRINT EXERCISES

EXERCISE 1: Family Questionnaire

As a family, talk together about the following family questions. Try to avoid making any negative comments about other people's ideas or insights. This is a time to listen to one another about your family life together.

- What do you like most about our family right now? Name several of your favorite family qualities.

- What do you like least about our family right now? Name several family traits you would like to change.

- Which best describes our family at the present?

    - Life-Together: regular time, daily and weekly spent together

    - Life-Apart: insufficient quality time spent together and too much time apart

    - Life-Without-Rules: too little guidance given to help the whole family

    - Life-on-the-Move: too many hours each week heading off somewhere else

- How do we balance our individual life and our family life together?

- How do I feel about the amount of time we are together and apart as a family?

- What do I think about the measure of freedom and discipline in this family?

- Do I feel our family is too home-bound or too much on the go?

EXERCISE 2: Family Survey

Assess where you are at the present time with your family. Some assessment involves measurable activities, such as number of meals shared per week. Some assessment involves your personal intuition about your family at present.

1. What about your family life do you appreciate most right now?

2. How often does your family meet together to plan, pray, and play?

Never Occasionally Monthly Weekly Daily

3. How much quality time each day do you spend with your child?

0 5 10 15 20 25 30 minutes

4. How many family meals do you share together each week?

1 2 3 4 5 6 7 8 9 10 or more meals

5. How often do you read aloud together with your children?

Never Occasionally Monthly Weekly Daily

6. How many hours per week is the TV on in your home?

Never under 5 hrs 5–10 hrs 10–20 hrs over 20 hrs

7. What changes in your family life would you like to make?

EXERCISE 3: Building Blocks for Parents

- Survey your approach to parenting, using building blocks drawn from the *Rule*.

- Mark your responses on a 1–5 scale as follows:
  *1= Never; 2 = Seldom; 3 = Occasionally;
  4 = Regularly; 5 = Almost Always*

- Circle several of the highest and star several of the lowest scores to review areas of strength and possible future growth in your approach to spiritual parenting.

A. __ A parent exemplifies the love of God in the family.

B. __ A parent points family members to all that is good more by example than by words.

C. __ Parents avoid all favoritism, but show equal love to everyone.

D. __ Parents do not gloss over troubles in the home, but weed them as soon as they begin to sprout.

E. __ Parents accommodate and adapt themselves to each child's character and intelligence.

F. __ Parents keep in mind that they have undertaken the care of souls.

G. __ Parents call the family together for regular family meetings.

H. __ A parent's way of life seeks to reflect the love of God to children.

I. __ Parents employ spiritual tools of love in the family.

J. ___ Parents keep due proportion between the seriousness of a fault and the measure of discipline.

K. ___ Parents exercise the utmost care and concern for the sick, the needy, and the hurting.

L. ___ Parents show every concern for the young, for guests, and the poor.

M. ___ Parents arrange all matters so that the family may go about activities without grumbling.

N. ___ Parents call the family together and lead the family in healthy spiritual habits.

O. ___ Parents seek to gain a treasury of spiritual knowledge from which they can draw.

P. ___ A parent is full of goodness of life and wisdom in teaching.

Q. ___ A parent is merciful, always letting "mercy triumph over judgment."

R. ___ Parents hate faults but love members of the family.

S. ___ Parents use wisdom and avoid extremes when training the family.

T. ___ Parents strive to be loved rather than feared, and love as they see best for each individual.

U. ___ Parents aren't excitable, anxious, obstinate, jealous or overly suspicious.

V. ___ Parents show forethought and consideration in giving orders and tasks.

W. __ Parents are discerning and moderate in leading others, using discretion.

X. __ Parents prefer nothing whatsoever to the love of God.

Y. __ Parents seek to follow God's paths with hearts overflowing with love.

Z. __ A parent relies upon God's help to guide the family towards their heavenly home.

EXERCISE 4: Planning Great Family Meetings

1. Call the family together

Set a regular time to meet together as a family. We found weekly or twice a month to be a good pattern. We also had a set night of the week for this family activity. Everyone is invited and expected to show up and participate. Plan meetings with the age level of your children in mind. With good planning, a great family meeting need only take 20 to 30 minutes.

Question for parents: How often does your family meet currently to discuss family life issues? What type of family meetings did you experience growing up? If this idea is something new to you, what type of family meeting would work well for your family life at this time? If you were to spend 30 minutes per week together as a family, sharing life at a family meeting, what would that half hour look like?

2. Serve up dessert for the family soul

Begin the family meeting with dessert, including sweets for the body and spiritual dessert for the soul. While family members are eating dessert, go around the table, asking everyone to offer a word of encouragement or praise for one other member of the family. Take a few minutes for words that build up the family and sweeten the soul. Share family stories from the day, pouring out words of encouragement and praise on family members.

Questions for parents: What is your family's favorite dessert? What do you think of the practice of each of your family members speaking words of encouragement to other family members at a meeting? At present, when does your family usually tell stories of their day? Who in your family tends to encourage family members to share stories and praise other family members?

3. Deal with family issues and decisions

Discuss a few family issues, asking for ideas on how to improve family life. Write decisions down in a family journal. Encourage everyone, even the youngest, to participate according to his or her ability. Make decisions by family consensus if possible, though parents always have final say. A word of encouragement: keep this section of the family meeting brief and upbeat so that family members will want to keep coming back to family meetings.

Questions for parents: How are family decisions currently being made? How do family members know what is expected of them? What are a few family issues facing your family at this time? How do you keep track of your family decisions, schedules and commitments?

4. Finish with family devotion

Have one member of the family light a candle. Try reading a short Bible story together. You may consider reading through one of the Gospels, story by story. After the Bible reading, consider holding hands in a circle and giving thanks to God for the many good gifts you've received. You may also conclude the family meeting by saying an ancient blessing to the family, such as "May God be gracious to us and bless us and make his face shine upon us."[11] During the week, follow up on any decisions you've made. Remind children through the week of any new family patterns or practices. Also, remind kids of the date and time for the next family meeting.

Questions for parents: What time of the week does your family currently share devotional life? If you currently do not have family devotions, what one new spiritual practice might you add into your family life this month? What simple prayers or devotional patterns did you grow up with or learn from your grandparents? What are the biggest obstacles to having family meetings in our home?

EXERCISE 5: Fifty-Two Family Construction Tools of Love

Below I've adapted the 73 Benedictine tools for good works (RB, 4) for the practice in the home, gathering them into months. I've also listed Bible references for families who want to read more about these tools. Try focusing upon a few tools each month, asking family members to put those tools to use in the family.

January

- Love God with all your heart, soul and strength (Luke 10:27).

- Love one another as God loves us (John 13:34).

- Clothe yourself with compassion, kindness, humility, gentleness and patience (Colossians 3:12).

- Develop the habit of giving and the spirit of gratitude (2 Corinthians 9:7).

- Practice honesty (Mark 10:19).

February

- Respect others (1 Peter 2:17).

- Live by the Golden Rule: "Do to others what you would have them do to you" (Matthew 7:12).

- Follow God as a "river guide" (Matthew 16:24).

- Learn to fast (Isaiah 58:6–7).

March

- Care for the needy in your community (Matthew 6:2–3).

- Clothe the poor (Matthew 25:36).

- Visit the sick (Matthew 25:36).

- Help out those who are troubled (Romans 12:20).

- Comfort the grieving (2 Corinthians 1:3–4).

April

- Avoid temptations (Luke 4:5-8).

- Bridle your anger and temper (Ephesians 4:26).

- Weed out any falsehood in your heart (Matthew 5:8).

- Practice peacemaking (Matthew 5:9).

May

- Always try to do what is right (Romans 12:17).

- Speak the truth in love (Ephesians 4:15).

- Do acts of kindness (1 Thessalonians 5:15).

- Patiently endure difficulties (Matthew 5:39).

- Live in harmony with others (Romans 12:16).

June

- Put love in action by caring for hurting people (Matthew 5:44).

- Speak well of people (1 Peter 3:9).

- Shine your light by doing a good deed (Matthew 5:16).

- Live moderately (Titus 1:7-8).

July

- Keep your spiritual fire going (Rom. 12:11).

- Offer hospitality (Romans 12:13).

- Avoid complaining and grumbling (Ephesians 4:31).

- Be quick to encourage others and build up one another (Ephesians 4:29).

August

* Find your soul's resting place in God (Psalm 62:1).
* Give thanks in every circumstance (1 Thessalonians 5:18).
* Take responsibility for the problems you see in your life (Psalm 51:2–3).
* Live more joyfully in the present (1 Thessalonians 5:16).
* Live a life of love (Ephesians 5:1).

September

* Keep watch over your actions and thoughts (Matthew 26:41).
* Give your anxieties to God (1 Peter 5:5–7).
* Remove trash talk from the home (Ephesians 5:4).
* Enjoy time meditating on the Bible (Colossians 3:16).

October

* Make prayer a heart habit (1 Thessalonians 5:18).
* Open your heart to God (Psalm 32:5).
* Grow spiritual fruit of love, joy and peace (Galatians 5:22).
* Respect others (Romans 13:7).

November

* Strive to live a spiritual life (Romans 12:1).
* Put your faith into action (Matthew 7:24–25).
* Seek God first and foremost (Matthew 6:33).
* Honor the elderly and care for the young (James 1:27).

December

- Make peace with others (Romans 12:18).

- Live in the shadow of God's mercy (Psalm 91:1–2).

- Go to sleep every night with a clear conscience (Psalm 4:4–8).

- Begin each new day with prayer to God (Psalm 5:1–3).

EXERCISE 6: Parenting as Spiritual Guidance

The following exercise invites parents to offer spiritual guidance to children. In addition to packing lunches, folding clothes, and paying bills, we are given the sacred task of walking alongside our children in their faith journey. Thus, spiritual guidance is one of the keys to spiritual parenting. There are a variety of ways to offer spiritual guidance to our children. Here is a list of possible approaches to parenting as spiritual guidance:

- Nurture spiritual fruit in the garden of your child's heart. Look for love, joy, peace, patience, kindness, goodness, gentleness, faithfulness, and self-control.[12]

- Prune back any "deadwood" you find in your life or in the life of your children.

- Encourage the fainthearted, the fearful, and the weary.

- Discern unique gifts and talents in your children.

- Share various responsibilities of leadership with children.

- Listen actively to your children, giving full attention to them, eye-to-eye and heart-to-heart.

- Teach your children about spiritual ways of living and practice them together.

- Allow God to love your children through you.

- Walk together with your children in their journey with God.

EXERCISE 7: Spirituality Questions for Parents

"Love God with all your heart and with all your soul and with all your strength. These commandments that I give you today are to be upon your hearts. Impress them on your children. Talk about them when you sit at home and when you walk along the road, when you lie down and when you get up. Tie them as symbols on your hands and bind them on your foreheads. Write them on the doorframes of your homes and on your gates."[13] Family spirituality is centered upon loving God as a family with our whole self in all situations of our daily life, including waking and sleeping, life at home and life on the go, in use of our hands and use of our minds, in our coming and going. Use the following questions to consider for bringing God into daily life.

1. What are some ways your family helped you grow spiritually during your childhood?

2. Name some faith activities that would help your family to grow spiritually this year?

3. What are the main hindrances or obstacles to your family spiritual life at this time?

4. When do you most often practice the spiritual life together as a family? When you sit at home with your children or when you walk along the road? When you lie down or when you arise? In your coming and going?

5. Choose one activity for your family life to practice together this season. Make a commitment for your family spiritual life together.

❧ Chapter Two ❧

Tend the Fire

Spiritual Practices and Rituals

Seven times a day I praise you.
—Psalm 119:164

When you visit a wood-heated home, the warmth embraces you as soon as you step through the front door. Without tending the spiritual "fire" in the home, a family can become like a house without heat in winter. In Jack London's classic short story *To Build a Fire,* set in the subzero Yukon Territory, survival depended upon the skill of fire-craft. Too many families today have not learned the skill of spiritual fire-craft. Many of the troubles found in homes today originate in the neglect of the inner life of the family.

When I was a young father, I made my first retreat to a monastery. I went for a week, seeking to spend time with God and learn how to care for my busy, weary soul. The first morning, I shuffled half-asleep across the cloister courtyard in what seemed like the middle of a foggy night. As I sat in the dark chapel surrounded by the sound of monks chanting the psalms, my soul began to awake for Vigils. The time was 4:15 in the morning. I wanted to go back to bed. Yet somewhere deep within, my spirit hungered for God. I sensed a great spiritual longing within my soul. To arise before dawn and direct my heart to God was a new experience. I found myself offering a simple prayer, "God, teach me to pray."[14] This became the cry of my heart. When we simply admit, "I do not know how to pray," from this beginning, we allow God to teach us as a family to draw close to God. Prayer is kindled by the spark of God's Spirit in our lives, igniting faith, hope, and love in the stove of family spirituality.

The fire of family spirituality needs to be tended daily just like a fire needs constant care. As with other tasks we try to accomplish during a day, we also need to give attention to our commitment to spiritual practices. In this chapter, we'll look at practical ways of inviting God to dwell in the family through the art of tending the family fire.

The Morning Spark

Benedict amuses me when he writes, *It seems reasonable to arise at the eighth hour of the night* (RB, 8). Nothing seems reasonable to me at four in the morning. I've heard the same from monks. Yet, in homes, just as in monasteries, family life often calls us to awake before the dawn, especially when we have young children. Like life in a monastery, family life is a training school in which we learn some important life lessons. One of our best spiritual teachers is morning time with God. This doesn't come naturally to most people, and is especially hard for night people like myself who seldom awaken before dawn.

Morning time with God sets the tone for the day. Before morning tasks, we first go to God. As parents, we nurture our children through our own morning time with God. There are no shortcuts in this classroom. We learn to pray by praying. We can read books about the spiritual life. This is not a bad idea, but it is not the same as prayer. After we've set aside time and place for morning time with God, after we've removed distractions and committed ourselves to time alone with God, we open our hearts to God.

Seek to develop the habit of morning time with God. We are wise to arise before our children, even before the break of the new day. I must confess that I feel inadequate writing this since I have great difficulty getting up early in the morning. Yet, two or three times a week, I drag myself out of bed before dawn to pray with others. As I've committed my life to morning time with God, I've noticed God's presence and guidance through the day. I've discovered greater patience with my family, greater clarity in my work, and greater enjoyment in my life with God and with my family. Dietrich Bonhoeffer, a twentieth-century German pastor and martyr, wrote about the benefit of morning time with God:

> The entire day receives order and discipline when it acquires unity. This unity must be sought and found in morning prayer. The morning prayer determines the day. Squandered time of which we

are ashamed, temptations to which we succumb, weaknesses and lack of courage in work, disorganization and lack of discipline in our thoughts and in our conversation with other men, all have their origin most often in the neglect of morning prayer.[15]

No greater adventure awaits us in this life than to start our day together with God. When we begin to make time for God in the morning, our hearts will spark into flames, bringing warmth to our children as they awaken into the new day.

Kindling to Get the Fire Going

Anyone who has ever started a fire knows the value of kindling. We need paper and small pieces of wood that will quickly ignite at the strike of a match. In the *Rule,* Benedict gives us simple practices that fuel the spiritual fire of the family: pray the Psalms, sing songs of faith, and read Scripture together.

Pray the Psalms

Psalms provide the busy family with prayers that have nurtured hearts for many generations. We can offer these ancient words as our own prayer to God and find that they voice our truths and our longings. The Psalms connect us with God and, like pieces of dry kindling, help get our fire going. Benedict advises us to begin the morning with the Psalms. For a simple way of praying

the Psalms, look at the *Exercises* section at the end of
this chapter.

Sing Spiritual Songs

Along with the Psalms, a second way to get the family fire going in the morning is singing songs of faith,
hope, and love. Our family loves to sing blessing songs
before family meals. I often play sacred music in the
morning, knowing that the first song heard in the morning is often carried through the day. In addition, try
singing songs to your children as they are waking up in
the morning. Better to wake up to the sound of music
than to wake up to alarms and buzzers. Years ago, while
still in high school, our middle son Stefan told us he
ran better during a hard cross-country practice because
he heard Vivaldi playing in his head. It was the music
I played that morning as he was getting up. There is
an abundance of great family music resources available,
both online, in CD recordings, and in print. Collect a
few of these and continue the ancient tradition of raising children with sacred music singing in their hearts
and in the home.[16]

Read Together

During breakfast, we've often read aloud from a book of
daily Scripture passages. Family morning reading need
not take a long time. Get a contemporary Bible translation and read a paragraph from one of the Gospels
during breakfast. Place a bookmark in the section where
you read so you can pick up in the same place the next
day. Some families conclude the reading with a short

prayer of thanks to God. These three spiritual practices, praying, singing, and reading, help rekindle the family spiritual fire in the morning.

Seasons of the Heart

In homes a century ago, the family gathering place was around the hearth or the wood stove, especially during the colder months. In homes today, technology has taken over the task of heating the home. With one touch we can regulate the temperature of the home, depending on the season. In the same way, spiritual life in the home needs to be regulated according to the season. In the *Rule* Benedict mentions winter and summer arrangements of the common life of prayer in the monastic family. These practical instructions reveal his gentle wisdom with regard to seasonal rhythms. Benedict's underlying assumption is that we dwell with God through the seasons and through the years. He understood that the spiritual life, much like the physical life, emerges through everyday life lived through the annual cycles of seasons.

Try developing family patterns of dwelling with God through the year. No matter what the season, we can keep the family spiritual fire going. Just as we regulate the temperature in our homes through the year, we are also wise to adjust our spiritual life as a family through the year. In this way, we discover new ways of participating in spiritual life together with God as a family.

Winter

During the winter, light a candle for meals or prayer times. Gather in a circle to sing, pray, and celebrate God's gift of light and warmth. Curl up with a wool blanket to read together stories of faith, hope, and love.

Spring

During the spring, encourage new growth in your family's spiritual life. Plant spiritual habits, and let the sunlight of God's love shine upon your family, enabling these habits to grow into fruitful daily practices.

Summer

During the summer, our spiritual life bears the sweet fruit of goodness, gentleness, and faithfulness. Share creative ways of knowing God with your children. Go on faith walks together to notice the design and wonder of creation.

Autumn

During the autumn, God's fruit is harvested for all to enjoy. As you return to the fall schedule after the summer, return to familiar patterns of spiritual practices, such as morning prayer and family fire starters. Find practical ways to serve one another in the day as an outward sign of God's fruitful way of life.

Vary the structure of family prayers according to the season of faith. Different seasons call for different spiritual habits. We don't need to get caught up in "shoulds" and "oughts." The spiritual life is not about guilt and regret, but about starting the fire of faith and keeping it burning through the year, allowing each season to call us back to God.

Rest and Recreation

Consider setting aside one day each week for family rest and recreation. We don't need to be too strict about this, but rather understand this weekly pattern as a guide for bringing us together into the fullness of life. For the past three thousand years, Jewish people have celebrated one day each week as distinct from the other six. Beginning every Friday evening, Jewish people honor God by keeping the Sabbath. This family practice is considered such an important habit that it is one of the Ten Commandments, the Bible's "top-ten" list.[17] Over the past two thousand years, Christians have also set aside one day of the week as distinct from the other six, celebrating Sundays as the Lord's Day, a day to celebrate the resurrection of Jesus from the grave. Though you may not have grown up in a Jewish or Christian home, consider a few reasons below for the practice of a weekly day of rest and recreation.

The Sabbath as Re-Creation

The first reason for keeping a weekly Sabbath is simply that this weekly habit helps to reunite us to God as our Creator. As the fourth commandment tells us: "Remember the Sabbath day by keeping it holy. For in six days the Lord made the heavens and the earth, the sea and all that is in them, but he rested on the seventh day. Therefore the Lord blessed the Sabbath day and made it holy."[18] In keeping a family day of rest, we are reminded that we are not the center of the universe. At the heart of creation is the Creator who established an order for the good of all creation. A weekly family day of rest invites us not only to enjoy leisure and recreation. This day is a weekly invitation to be re-created by God, to have our lives renewed inwardly. Many busy families fill their weekends with recreational activities. A busy weekend filled with many leisure activities can be exhausting and become a shallow substitute for true spiritual renewal found in the heart of God. This is the first great purpose behind a weekly family day of rest.

The Sabbath as Restoration

The second reason for keeping a weekly family day of rest is to restore our lives and free us from unhealthy lifestyles. As the fourth commandment declares, "Observe the Sabbath day by keeping it holy. Remember that you were slaves in Egypt and that the Lord your God brought you out of there with a mighty hand and an outstretched arm."[19] In keeping a family Sabbath we accept that we have gotten snared and even enslaved by unhealthy ways of living including self-centeredness, busyness, materialism, and over-scheduling. A family Sabbath day invites us to celebrate God's work of restoring our lives, releasing us from any kind of slavery or addictive living. Enjoying a family day of rest and re-creation can help return our focus on the essential things of life and restore us to the fullness of life. In today's busy world, it may be a challenge to add such a day of rest and recreation into our week as a family.

Schedules, athletic events, school homework, paying the bills and other family demands can pull members of the family in different directions. How then to add Sabbath time to your family? Here are three creative ideas for a family day of rest and recreation: weekly worship, family adventures, and family devotion.

Weekly Worship

Creating a meaningful habit of worship is like learning to play a musical instrument. Few people can play the piano on the first try and make a beautiful sound. Over months of practice, we begin to make pleasing music. Attending worship together may be compared to going to music lessons. With God as our music teacher, we learn the basic scales of the faith and have hands-on opportunity to practice what we've learned through the week. Elements of worship include songs, prayers, and study. In song we raise our voices and hearts to God. Through prayer we enjoy friendship with God. Through study of Scripture, we learn more of God's heart and purposes for our lives. I've known a number of families where one parent did not participate in faith activities. Often, after a time, the non-believing parent has come to appreciate the bright influence of faith, hope, and love in their child. Looking through a child's trusting eyes has a beautiful way of drawing parents into the circle of God's love.

Family Adventures

For another creative way to enjoy a family day of recreation, consider surprising the family by planning a weekend activity that carries the family into a new place. These activities can be in tune with the seasons or based on something else important to your family. A few seasonal ideas include:

Enjoy a Spring walk around the neighborhood to observe the new growth of buds on trees and flowers in gardens. Take along a set of binoculars and go bird watching. If you have a bird book, mark the birds you've seen in the index and read together about their habits and habitats.

In the Summer, take the family on overnight camping trips and enjoy family time outdoors, with campfire songs around the fire, roasted s'mores, and nature walks in the forest or along the beach.

In the Autumn, visit a "U-pick" orchard or farm where you can enjoy the time of harvest, bringing home fresh fruit and vegetables. Rake leaves in your yard and put up fall decorations.

In Winter, take a trip to the library to pick out some new books. Consider playing your own family version of "Are You Smarter than a Fifth Grader?" to encourage your children to present what they've been learning in school. Ask children to come up with their own ideas for the next family recreation day activity. Make a list and begin to add fun, learning, and spirituality to your family weekend.

Family Devotion

Sometimes as a family we've gotten up too late for worship at a local church. Benedict was aware of the human tendency to be late: *This arrangement should be followed*

*at all times, summer and winter, unless . . . the members
happen to arise too late.* When such occurs in the monastery, Benedict offers a moderate solution: *In that case
the readings will have to be shortened* (RB, 11). In the
spirit of Benedict, be flexible and gracious regarding
family approaches to worship. One of the best ways to
celebrate the Sabbath as a family is to plan for a time on
Saturday or Sunday for family devotions.

* Gather the family together.

* Have a child light a candle.

* Read aloud a part of a Psalm or a portion of the
  Gospels.

* Provide paper and color markers for children to draw
  what they are thinking about.

* Take a few minutes for a time of quiet family
  reflection.

* Sing a song or hymn together.

* Offer a prayer of thanks.

Such home-style worship offers a family a lovely alternative to many busy events and activities outside the
home on a weekend. Rest and recreation is God's gift
to the family. This weekly pattern was given to bring
renewal and refreshment. The Sabbath is a family celebration day, a day of rest and a day of returning, a day
of re-creation and restoration in our God.

Holidays and Holy Days

In every season, there are many opportunities to plan special family celebrations. In our home, we have always loved celebrating birthdays and national holidays such as the Fourth of July. In addition to ordinary celebrations in the home, *life-together* families make an effort to celebrate holy days in ways that children can understand and enjoy. Our English word "holiday" comes from "holy day," or a day set apart to celebrate God's presence in our midst. Such days are not just intended to be celebrated in church buildings or public places, but are meant to be enjoyed in homes. On holy days we remember God's great acts of love from the past. Benedict encourages the monastic family to celebrate special holidays including *the feasts of saints, and all festivals* (RB, 14). These festivals and holidays change from family to family, and families tend to develop their own special customs and traditions through the years. Here are a few of the more familiar holy days including some creative ideas to celebrate them as a family.

Advent

During this month-long season we celebrate the coming of God.[20] In our family, we light Advent candles in a wreath on Sunday evenings, one for each Sunday of the four weeks of Advent. Often included in our candle lighting are short readings from the Bible, a few Christmas carols, and family prayers. During this season of preparation, we decorate our home, bake nut breads to share with the neighbors, and make Christmas crafts, such as our own homemade wrapping paper or cut-out snowflakes for the windows. We also put out our Nativity Scene, placing the shepherds in one room, the wise men in another, and Mary and Joseph in a third. When our children were young they moved the shepherds and the wise men a little every day, until at last they stood by Mary and baby Jesus in the stable. One of our children's favorite daily activities during Advent was to open a small wrapped package on a homemade Advent calendar. These little gifts reminded them of the sweet gift of God's love at Christmas.

Christmas

On Christmas Eve, we join with our church family for a candlelight service of carols celebrating Jesus' birth. I've known families who bake a birthday cake on Christmas and give presents to the poor in celebration of Jesus' birth. On Christmas Eve, Mary and Joseph finally arrive at the stable in our Nativity scene, and Jesus is "born" in the manger. On Christmas Day, the shepherds arrive. Many families enjoy unique Christmas customs from around the world. My wife and her Danish mother have blessed our family with Danish Christmas customs. As part of our Christmas celebration, on Christmas Eve, we dance around the Christmas tree, holding hands and singing carols, and then dance through every room in the house with the whole house lit only by candlelight. All this happens before we sit down on Christmas Eve to exchange gifts.

Epiphany

On January 6th, we light candles to remember the Light of God that comes into the world. On this special day, known as Epiphany, the wise men of our Nativity scene finally bring their gifts to the baby Jesus in the manger. Epiphany is celebrated in many Spanish-speaking countries as Three Kings Day, in honor of the visit of the Magi from the East. We take down our Christmas decorations, sing Christmas carols one last time, and share a special holiday treat called the "King's Bread." An almond is hidden in one part of the bread. Whoever gets the almond gets to be king or queen for a day, wear a crown, and receive a gift, usually a box of chocolates.

Lent

Lent is a forty-day season of spiritual renewal. The word *lent* comes from an Old English word for "lengthening" of days, another word for Spring. During these forty days, we remember that Jesus fasted for forty days in the wilderness. Lent calls us to turn away from self-indulgent ways of living and return to God. During this time we encourage members of our family to consider what negative practices they might give up and what positive practices they might add as a new healthy habit during this springtime season.

Holy Week

Palm Sunday marks the beginning of Holy Week. On this Sunday, we recall the triumphal entry of Jesus into Jerusalem. A fun activity as a family may include a parade around the house on Palm Sunday, singing joyful songs to God in each room of the house. During Holy Week Christians celebrate the Lord's Supper on Holy Thursday, a time to remember the meal Jesus shared with his people the night before his death. During Holy Week, we also remember the death of Jesus on the cross on Good Friday. We've often used our Christmas tree to draw a connection between Christmas and Good Friday. After Christmas, we store the tree outside until Good Friday. Then we remove the branches and transform it into a cross. We bring the cross back into the house and set it up in our living room. On Easter morning, we have sometimes covered the cross with flowers, symbolizing the abundant new life of the resurrection.

Easter

On Easter we attend an outdoor sunrise service, singing joyful songs and raising a festal shout together. We also celebrate Easter together with a "flowering of the cross" processional during an indoor Easter worship service. An old wooden cross, covered with mesh wire, is transformed into a beautiful bouquet of spring flowers. As a family we decorate Pysanky Easter eggs together almost every year. This Ukrainian style of Easter egg requires the use of special dyes, beeswax candles, and a stylus called a *Kistka*. After several hours together designing and dyeing our Ukrainian Easter eggs, all the egg treasures are set out on egg holders to celebrate the coming of God's gift of new life in the resurrection.[21]

Pentecost

At Pentecost we welcome the coming of God's Spirit and new life. Since Pentecost usually comes in May, we celebrate the blossoming of springtime and the birthday of the Church, sometimes with a special party. Pentecost is also a great day for a bonfire to commemorate the flames of God's Spirit that came upon the first Christians.

All Saints' Day. The first day of November, "All Saints' Day," honors the lives of heroes of faith who walked before us. I like reading from Butler's *Lives of the Saints,* or from *All Saints* by Robert Ellsberg; these two books offer biographical readings for every day of the year. We offer our children a lasting gift when we introduce them to great people of faith, and thus find encouragement for our spiritual journey as a family. Many families also celebrate individual feast days through the year in remembrance of people who lived lives dedicated to God. Some of these saints have found their way into our national celebrations, such as St. Valentine's Day (February 14), St. Patrick's Day (March 17), and All Saints' Eve, or Halloween (October 31).

According to the meaning of each special day, we feast or fast, we gift thanks to God or cry out to God for help, we humbly bow our heads or lift up our eyes with joy. An excellent resource for entering into the sacred cycle of celebrations as a family is Gertrud Mueller Nelson's book, *To Dance with God: Family Ritual and Community Celebration.* Of such family celebrations, Nelson writes:

We mark the major moments in our human exis-
tence with a rite or a ceremony. Sometimes even
the smaller events in our lives need the recognition
of a celebration or the consciousness that a ritual
brings. In our creative ritual making we draw a
circle around that place and that event so that we
can be more fully awake to the magnitude of the
moment.[22]

When we mark our year by such holy days, we make
room in our lives for God's presence. Not only are we
remembering the past, we are playfully and prayerfully
entering God's ongoing drama in our world today. We
leave behind the life of the spectator and become actors
with God. What fun it is to bring our children into
these holy times year by year, joining with the Psalmist
who wrote of holy days long ago, "We will not hide
them from our children; we will tell the next generation
the praiseworthy deeds of the Lord, his power, and the
wonders he has done."[23]

Practice the Presence of God

One of the great lessons I've learned at my annual retreats at the monastery is the practice of the presence
of God. According to Benedict, seven times a day is
not too often to enjoy time with God. Monasteries now
gather three to five times a day to enjoy time together
with God. Besides the organized times of prayer, monks
also learn to practice the presence of God throughout

the day and night. *We believe that the divine presence is everywhere* (RB, 19).

One of the best-loved writers on prayer, Brother Lawrence, a French monk of the seventeenth century, writes of the benefit of taking small moments to return our hearts to God in his classic, *The Practice of the Presence of God.*

> God does not ask much of us. During your meals or during any daily duty, lift your heart up to him, because even the least little remembrance will please him. You don't have to pray out loud; he's nearer than you can imagine. It isn't necessary that we stay in church in order to remain in God's presence. We can make our heart a chapel where we can go anytime to talk to God privately. These conversations can be so loving and gentle, and anyone can have them.[24]

One of the struggles busy families face is finding the balance between activities outside the home and family time together inside the home. Brother Lawrence's vision of prayer as "practicing the presence of God" has helped me as a parent more regularly reorient my life towards God, by simply and gently recognizing the presence of God in the midst of busy family life. Here are a few examples of ways to practice the presence of God:

- During the crazy time just before leaving to school, stop for a minute and acknowledge God's presence with your family;

- Hold hands in a circle and offer a short silent or spoken prayer together at restaurants after athletic events in neighboring towns;

- Transform the family car or van into a sacred place filled with God's presence as you quietly pray for your children before they hop out into the next activity.

For more creative ideas on practicing God's presence, see the *Exercises* at the end of this chapter. As we take up Lawrence's simple habit of practicing the presence of God, no matter if we are coming or going, God's presence will continue to ignite our lives and we'll have spiritual warmth and compassion to share with our children and their friends.

The Heart of Prayer

Early in my vocation as a pastor, I found my prayer life filled with busyness, distractions, and gnawing anxiety. In October 1986, while on a week-long spiritual retreat, I met with Peter, a monk at the abbey near our home. I explained to him that I wasn't spending much quality time with God. Peter described prayer as a light weight raft, easily carried through the day, a raft upon which I could cross over into the presence of God at anytime. He taught me a simple ancient prayer: Lord, have mercy (Greek: *Kyrie Eleison*). Peter encouraged me to unite this simple prayer to the rhythm of my breathing. My life has never been the same since. Thanks to Peter, I discovered the heart of prayer.

Benedict writes of prayer: *We must know that God regards our purity of heart and tears of compunction, not our many words. Prayer should therefore be short and pure* (RB, 20). According to Benedict, prayer is powerful, capable of transforming our lives. For this very reason, the world is full of prayer substitutes. Instead of prayer from the heart, many people fill their lives with wordy prayers or pretense prayers, prayer substitutes that have little power to change us. Like trying to satisfy our hunger with candy, such prayer substitutes will leave us with an even greater spiritual hunger.

God loves to meet us where we are and teach us to pray. When we pray from the heart, we open our lives to God, like opening the front door of our homes to a close friend. Wise parents teach their children to pray in such a manner. Prayer is more than merely reciting religious-sounding words and phrases. Prayer is intimacy with God. When we pray, our lives will be transformed. The reward of true prayer is found in the delight of intimacy with God. Like building a fire in a wood stove, family spirituality may be understood as the heart and hearth of the home. Through the practices and principles in this chapter, families learn to maintain the fire of spirituality. Around this hearth, others will gather to find warmth and friendship with our family and with God.

FAMILY SPIRITUALITY EXERCISES

EXERCISE 1: Morning Time with God

"Very early in the morning, while it was still dark, Jesus got up, left the house and went off to a solitary place, where he prayed."[25] Taking our lead from Jesus' example of praying in the morning, try out some of the following patterns for morning prayer.

1. Wake up prayer. Try waking up to sacred or classical music instead of digital buzzers or electric alarms. Let the first sound you hear in the morning be beautiful music that feeds the soul.

2. Shower prayer. Envision the shower stall as a sacred prayer place where you connect up with God with nothing to hide, honest and truly unclothed. Allow God's goodness and love to wash over you.

3. Clothing prayer. As you clothe yourself in the morning, offer your life to God by clothing yourself "with compassion, kindness, humility, gentleness and patience."[26] Put on these virtues in the morning.

4. Coffee prayer. Try sitting still for a few minutes in the morning, holding a cup of coffee, and soaking in the silence of the new day. If you like, put on some peaceful music. Listen. Meditate. Be still. Practice God's presence. This too is prayer. It is strengthening for you to take this time before kids wake up.

5. Waking children. Not many parents are professional singers, but all children love hearing their
parents sing. Why not waken our children with
songs? Consider singing prayer songs to them as
they waken into the new day. There are many
simple, ancient prayer songs such as *Dona Nobis
Pacem, Ubi Caritas,* and *Jubilate Deo.* We've sung
these to our kids for years.

6. Written morning prayer. Open a child-friendly
prayer book and read aloud a written prayer when
your children sit down for breakfast. The best
prayer book is the *Book of Psalms.*

7. Taxi prayer. Most parents spend plenty of time
driving kids in the morning. Why not transform
some of this time in the car into time with God?
Without any fanfare, bells or neon lights, quietly
offer your heart's gratitude to God for your
children riding in the car with you. Ask God to
guide your kids and help them grow in body,
mind, and spirit. As your children hop out to head
off to school, bless your children saying, "God
bless your day; I love you."

EXERCISE 2: Praying the Psalms

Our home is surrounded by a forest of trees. Every window of our home looks out into the green wonder of the
forest. Like windows looking into an ancient forest, the
Book of Psalms reveals the wonder and beauty of meditation and prayer. Return again and again to this sacred
grove through the well-traveled path of praying the

Psalms. For nearly three thousand years, families have turned to the Psalms as their family guide to prayer. We are wise today to affirm the ancient spiritual habit of praying the Psalms.

The "Five Friends" approach to praying the Psalms

• Pray the Psalms by reading them aloud in the home according to the day of the month.

• On the first day of the month, five Psalms await the family, including Psalm 1, 31, 61, 91 and 121.

• On the second day of the month, choose from Psalm 2, 32, 62, 92 or 122.

• Choose from every thirtieth Psalm according to the day of the month.

• Continue through the month in this manner, praying one or more of the Psalms of the day as if they were spiritual friends teaching you to pray.

• On the 30th of the month, pray Psalm 30, 60, 90, 120 or 150.

• Psalm 119, the longest Psalm and also the longest chapter in the Bible with 176 verses, deserves its own day. Save this Psalm for the months with 31 days. On the 31st, pray through the stanzas in Psalm 119.

• In this way, you will survey the Psalms each month, and deepen your family life with God.

• Beware of getting caught up in trying to perfect some spiritual system or technique. As Benedict wisely counsels, *If people find this distribution of the psalms unsatisfactory, they should arrange whatever they judge better* (RB, 18).

◆ The goal is intimacy with the living God through praying the Psalms as a family.

◆ God gives us these 150 spiritual friends to guide us into a life of intimacy with God.

EXERCISE 3: The Lord's Prayer

A baby's first word is a beautiful moment in parenting. Human speech is a skill learned over years of daily instruction. Like learning a language, children also need to be taught how to pray. The basic prayer in family spirituality is the prayer Jesus taught, known as "The Lord's Prayer," or the "Our Father." Simone Weil, the modern French philosopher, writes of this prayer,

> The "Our Father" contains all possible petitions; we cannot conceive of any prayer not already contained in it. It is to prayer what Christ is to humanity. It is impossible to say it once through, giving the fullest possible attention to each word, without a change, infinitesimal perhaps but real, taking place in the soul.[27]

Praying this prayer, we admit to ourselves and to God that we do not know how to pray. We are beginners at prayer and life-long students of prayer. The family is a school for prayer in which parents teach their children and children teach us as parents how to pray. This simple prayer is for the family. Every phrase expresses the deepest yearnings of every family. In your family, recite one phrase for each day of the week.

◆ Sunday: Our Father, who art in heaven, hallowed be Thy name.

◆ Monday: Thy kingdom come, thy will be done on earth as it is in heaven.

◆ Tuesday: Give us this day our daily bread.

◆ Wednesday: Forgive us our trespasses as we forgive those who trespass against us.

◆ Thursday: Lead us not into temptation.

◆ Friday: But deliver us from evil.

◆ Saturday: For Thine is the kingdom and the power and the glory, forever, Amen.

Benedict prescribes praying this prayer in the monastic family daily. *Assuredly, the celebration of Lauds and Vespers must never pass by without the abbot reciting the entire Prayer of Jesus at the end for all to hear* (RB, 13). As families regularly recite the Lord's Prayer together, children will quickly learn this prayer by heart, and carry it in their hearts the rest of their days. This prayer is a deep well. The family that comes often to drink from this well will enjoy a lifetime of spiritual refreshment in God.

EXERCISE 4: Family Prayer Places

Throughout history, people have set aside special places for being alone with God. Moses went up onto a mountain. David went into the sanctuary. Mary pondered God's mysteries in her own heart. Jesus loved the garden of Gethsemane. The same is true with Benedict in the sixth century: *The oratory [the prayer chapel] ought to be what it is called, and nothing else is to be done or stored there* (RB, 52). Every family needs sacred places for prayer. Benedict understood the reality of busy family life in the monastery. Thus, he set apart a special place and special times for quiet prayer. No one is to be disturbed while praying: *All should leave in complete silence and with reverence for God, so that anyone who may wish to pray alone will not be disturbed by the insensitivity of another. If at other times some choose to pray privately, they may simply go in and pray, not in a loud voice, but with tears and heartfelt devotion* (RB, 52). Here then are a dozen creative ways to make space for prayer in your home and family life together.

Family prayer places

1. Pour a bath.

2. Set aside a chair in a quiet corner by a window.

3. Transform an unused closet into a little prayer room.

4. Use a kneeling bench.

5. Sit on a woven rug and go for a childlike "carpet ride" into the presence of God.

6. Sit on a bench in a corner of the garden.

7. Lean against a tree on your property or somewhere near your home.

8. Get away during a lunch break to an empty church sanctuary for prayer.

9. Turn your car into a place of gratitude and prayer while sitting at traffic lights.

10. Hang a hammock on a covered deck and hang out with God.

11. Kneel by your bedside.

12. Make your heart a chapel. As Brother Lawrence suggests, "It isn't necessary that we stay in church in order to remain in God's presence. We can make our heart a chapel where we can go anytime to talk to God privately."[28]

In these places we offer our lives to God, alert to the whispering voice of God. In these places, enter the sanctuary of God's Spirit, and quietly enjoy being with God. From the place of prayer, we leave refreshed and transformed by God's goodness and love.

EXERCISE 5: The Fire-Craft of Family Spirituality

The following exercise involves building a fire as a symbol of family spiritual life. If you do not have a fireplace or woodstove in your home, consider building a fire outdoors in a fire pit at a local park or in a BBQ grill in the backyard. Three basic elements of family spirituality are emphasized in this exercise. To build a fire, all three elements are needed.

Fuel

First, have a child put crumpled up paper and small pieces of wood kindling into the fireplace or fire pit.

Have some wood logs ready to add to the fire once the fire is going well. For family spirituality, the fuel is God's wisdom and truth found in the Bible. Enjoy opening the Scriptures as a family. If you have younger children, read aloud from a children's Bible. Bookstores and publishing companies offer many great resources for Scripture time with children. Ask teachers, grandparents and other parents for recommendations of the best resources to fuel your family fire. Choose out a few and try them out in your family for a month.

Spark

Without a spark, a fire will never start. Get out a box of matches. Ask a child to help you strike the match and light paper on fire. It may take several matches, several sparks to ignite the family fire. The spark of family spirituality is faith, hope, and love expressed through prayer. Just as the flames ignite the dry wood, as we turn our hearts to God, our hearts are rekindled with God's great love. Our children teach us to pray and help spark our faith in God. Listen to the prayers of your children. Try reading aloud from written prayers that draw upon the faith and wisdom of people who have gathered around the fire of God's love before us. Pray for each member of the family, that you all will grow in love.

Oxygen

Once the fire has begun to catch flame, show your children how to fan the fire. Like fanning the flames in a newly lit fire, we add to our family spirituality the wind of God's Spirit through singing songs of faith. Young children love to sing. Sing all kinds of songs, including faith songs as a regular part of your home life together. Get CDs of songs appropriate to the age of your children. Find age-appropriate songbooks you can use as a family to sing together. Close your family time around the fire you've built by singing a few campfire songs that unite your family in heart and voice.

EXERCISE 6: Practice the Presence of God

Here's a list of quotes from Brother Lawrence's *The Practice of the Presence of God*. I've adapted these quotes for the family. Try posting some of these on your refrigerator or bringing them up as topics for family conversation. Circle your favorites.

- Resolve to make the love of God the motive of all family actions.

- Do little things in the home for the love of God.

- Our primary family business is to love and delight ourselves in God.

- Seek to be with God moment by moment.

- Do not be weary of doing little things in the home for the love of God, who regards not the greatness of the work, but the love with which it is performed.

- Never be hasty, but try to do each thing in its season, with an even, uninterrupted composure and tranquility of spirit.

- The time of chores does not differ from the time of prayer; and in the noise and clutter of busy family life, seek to possess God in as great tranquility as if resting quietly in God's love.

- In the height of family busyness, seek to drive away everything that interrupts being in God's presence.

- The spiritual life is a gift from God.

- We often hinder God and stop the flow of God's love. But when God finds a family with a lively faith, God pours out favors plentifully.

- Those who have the wind of God's Spirit go forward even in sleep.

- God is nearer to us in our homes than we are aware of.

- Retire from time to time to converse with God in meekness, humility, and love.

- Don't go faster than God's love. One does not become spiritual all at once.

- Our only business in this life is to please God.

- God loves us infinitely more than we imagine.

- Make the heart of our family a spiritual temple wherein to enjoy God at all times.

- Love God equally in pains and pleasures.

- That practice which is alike the most spiritual, the most practical, and the most needful in the home is the practice of the presence of God.

- God is within us. Do not seek God elsewhere.

- The presence of God is thus the life and nourishment of the family soul.

EXERCISE 7: Praying Through the Day

Benedict offered the monastic family seven times each day for time with God, beginning early in the morning before dawn, and finishing at night. This exercise offers parents a way for families to begin learning to pray through the day.

1. When you awake, offer the new day to God and pray a Psalm together.

2. While bathing in the morning, open your life to God and ask God to wash your inner life as the shower washes your body.

3. Give thanks to God as a family before you eat breakfast.

4. Take a few deep breaths and breathe in God's goodness during a morning break.

5. At lunchtime, bow your head to offer thanks to God. We encouraged our school-age children to say a silent lunchtime prayer of thanks before eating lunch.

6. Hold hands around the dinner table to receive God's gift of food and life.

7. At bedtime, recite the Lord's Prayer together or say a childhood prayer such as, "Now I lay me down to sleep, I pray the Lord my soul to keep." After

your children are asleep, just before you turn in for the night, go into your child's room, rest your hand upon your child's head, and offer thanks to God for such an amazing gift. Then go to bed and sleep in peace. God works the night shift.

Chapter Three

Stretch and Strengthen

Training the Family Team

Train up a child in the way he should go, and when he is old he will not turn from it.

— Proverbs 22:6

Family spirituality may be compared to participating in team sports or in other group activities that involve training together. Even if your children are not involved with sports, you most likely drive them to team-like activities, such as dance lessons, band practice or theater rehearsal. Family spiritual life involves training together with people who are focused upon the same goals. The Bible describes parenting as team training, as seen in the following instructions from St. Paul. "Fathers, do not make your children angry, but raise them with the training and teaching of the Lord."[29] Benedict also emphasizes training in the monastic family, encouraging monks to progress in the spiritual life through faithful training. Sounding like a long-distance running coach, he encourages us to train well for the race of faith. *As we progress in this way of life, we shall run on the path of God's commandments, our hearts overflowing with the inexpressible delight of love* (RB, prologue). In this chapter we will look at Benedict's training advice for the family and see how parents can coach their families with the goal of becoming a healthy, spiritual team.

Playing as a Team

In a healthy family, members work together as a team. A few years ago, on the day our sons arrived home from college for the summer, I put up a new kitchen chore chart on the door of the fridge that declared, "Stefan and Thomas do everything!" We shared a laugh over this and then set about integrating them into the schedule of jobs to be done. In our home no one is expected to do everything. We all share in caring for our home. Though our college sons hadn't done many chores during their semester away at school, as soon as they rejoined our household they were expected to participate in the upkeep of the house.

When it comes to motivating kids to do chores, our family has had its struggles like most every other home. Neglecting to do what we promised is a problem in most homes. Still, over the years, we've tried to hold each other accountable to do these tasks. Washing dishes and clothes, cleaning bedrooms and bathrooms, weeding the garden and feeding pets: all these chores teach our kids to care for themselves, care for others, and care for the earth. Through such instruction children learn healthy life habits and the importance of responsible stewardship.

The family team is strengthened by players who share responsibility according to their age and ability. Benedict says *Let the [family members] serve each other so that no one be excused from the work in the kitchen* (RB, 35). In the *life-together* family, no one is exempt from chores. The less desirable duties such as cleaning the bathroom or taking out garbage are tasks that we share in a rotation schedule so that no one is burdened with an unpleasant task for too long. To liven things up we've enjoyed holding a family "chore draft day," where we placed all the jobs, written on little pieces of paper, into a hat and have family members draw out their chores for the season.

Our role as parents is not only to share responsibility with our children, but to train them how to fulfill these responsibilities and expect them to accomplish the tasks we've given them. Along with their chores, children need instruction, encouragement, and loving accountability to fulfill their duties. One of the most challenging aspects of parenting is the ongoing work of teaching children how to do simple tasks, and then checking and rechecking that these tasks are accomplished. Usually it is easier to do the job ourselves.

We've found it helpful to praise our children when they complete their chores. Offer your thanks and commendations when children have fulfilled what they set out to do. Benedict reminds us that people matter more than things. Better a joyful family in a cluttered house than a grumpy family in a spotless house. Try to encourage a playful, supportive spirit when doing chores. Benedict warns against grumbling, and instead promotes an attitude of gratitude, kindness and joyful service in the home.

Good Sportsmanship

Many children today grow up without being trained to respect others. This disrespect can include bad attitudes towards parents and other adults. Children who learn good sportsmanship from their parents will grow in health and goodness. A serious danger arises in the home when children have disrespect for parental training. Such disrespect shows up in the voice, face, or body language. In our home, we have not allowed back-talk, snide remarks, or other disrespectful forms of speech, even from friends who are visiting. We also employed a "zero-tolerance" approach to acts of disrespect or physical violence in the home. When children learn the heart of respect in the home, this gift is carried out into schools, soccer fields, workplaces, and neighborhoods.

Children who engage in disrespectful speech or actions are testing the strength and boundaries of family training. We all want to feel loved and protected. At the same time, we strive for independence and freedom. These two powerful urges often conflict in the souls of our children. When our kids are disrespectful they are asking to be loved and trained in the way of good sportsmanship. Parents who neglect to show respect for one another or for their children infect the life of their family with an inner sickness.

Even served with love, certain forms of family training can taste unpleasant. As Scripture affirms, "No
discipline seems pleasant at the time, but painful. Later
on, however, it produces a harvest of righteousness and
peace for those who have been trained by it."[30] One of
the difficult tasks we have as parents is to seek the best
healing treatment for our children and to allow time
for that treatment to work. Sometimes, inner troubles
need time and professional treatment to heal. Parents
who place a high value on respect in the home assure
their children they are loved and highly valued and
such homes nurture healthy, loving children. Parents
who nurture a spirit of good sportsmanship on the family team know that the health of the family is a gift
from God, a gift arising from hearts of mutual love and
respect.

Delay of Game

Every autumn, from the time they were young children into their teenage years, our three sons gathered
up cleats and shin guards, piled into the car and we
drove north for soccer practice. I don't remember how
many times we left the house late, hoping not to get
pulled over for speeding on our way to soccer practice.
As a family, we've been known to be late to practices
on more than a few occasions.

   Parents are responsible for planning the family schedule and calling the family together. Children are responsible for showing up on time. Tardiness is a common

problem for most families. In many team sports, players who delay the game face a penalty. Applying such
a "team-sport" approach to the tardiness in the family
can strengthen the family team. Benedict highly valued
members of the monastic family sitting down together
for meals and offering together a table grace before each
meal. When monks show up late for a meal, the whole
community pays a price. Thus, Benedict warns those
who hold the community back because of lateness. *If
monastics do not come to table before the verse so that all
may say the verse and pray and sit down at table together,
and if this failure happens through their own negligence or
fault, they should be reproved . . .* (RB, 43).

According to Benedict, keep showing up late for
meals and you'll eat by yourself for a time. If anyone
arrives late at family gatherings, that person has cost the
family a small price. The tardy person shall also pay a
small price. Reasonable consequences for tardiness may
include the following:

- last to the table is last to be served;
- last to get ready for school is last to invite friends
  over after school;
- last to pick up his or her mess is first to take out
  the trash;
- last to bed is first to be sent to bed the next night;
- last to the car is last to choose a seat.

In the face of tardy behavior, there is little need for
angry words or threats. Our children need bowls of
encouragement and cups of lectures. Remind kids gently

about how much time until the "tardy buzzer" goes off. If the tardy behavior persists, sound the "buzzer" and remove privileges. "Delay of game" deprives the family of unity. Especially at family meal times everyone in our home is expected to show up on time. Sitting together for meals is a healthy family habit. Such unhealthy habits as eating on the run, eating in shifts, eating in different rooms, coming late for common meals: these can be overcome through gentle, consistent training.

When we gather together at home, we're preparing our children for a lifetime of showing up on time at school, in the community, and at work. Ultimately, we are training our children for the great banquet being prepared for all God's children in the age to come. Therefore, "let us not give up meeting together, as some are in the habit of doing, but let us encourage one another — and all the more as you see the Day approaching."[31]

Team Laundry

If your kids play team sports, they'll be sure to come home with dirty laundry. *Life-together* families deal with dirty laundry by training the family to take responsibility for cleaning up their messes. When I speak of dirty laundry, I mean more than merely soiled clothes, but also unloving actions, unkind attitudes, and soiled souls. Part of raising children involves "doing team laundry" by facing mistakes honestly and practicing loving accountability and forgiveness.

Benedict taught his family of monks to make amends for their mistakes. *Should anyone make a mistake ... he*

must make satisfaction there before all (RB, 45). Part of
playing on a team involves making mistakes together. In
high school basketball, we were told to make up for our
mistakes by playing with even greater intensity at the
other end of the court. As parents, we've asked ourselves
how to build up our kids when they made mistakes.
We've tried to help them not only experience the consequences of their decisions but also find creative ways
to learn from their mistakes. Like most families, we are
a work in progress.

In the family team there are always messes to clean
up. We all make mistakes and need training to learn to
wash up after ourselves. As parents, we too are accountable for our thoughts, attitudes, and deeds in parenting.
Our children are watching us to see how we live out the
principles and guidelines we've spoken. Our mistakes
offer plenty of opportunities to train the family in the
way of love by example. When we walk with arrogance,
denial, or self-pity after making a mistake, we only add
to our troubles. More mistakes do not correct the original mistake. Better to bring the first mistake into the
light of love and responsibly show our children how to
"do the laundry" through forgiveness and love.

Benedict assumes that people will make mistakes, but
expects that when mistakes are made that they will
be dealt with in a wise and loving manner. We can
complain about our children's dirty clothes. Or we can
accept the ongoing labor of love, train our children to
play as a team, and learn to do team laundry. When a
family is unfettered by piles of "dirty laundry" such as

unresolved conflict and messes, they have the opportunity to face each new day in a way that is fresh and free. There is a quiet joy to be found in honestly facing family troubles, and seeing our beautiful children step out into the new day dressed in clean clothes.

Coaching Tips for Parents

Parents and coaches have a lot in common. Like good coaches, parents build team confidence by inspiring every family member to strive for excellence on and off the field. We heap encouragement and praise upon our "team," yet are also unafraid to challenge the family when needed. We find ways to motivate our children to strive for excellence in all they do and are always looking for ways to improve the "team spirit" of the family.

Great coaches know how to build team character, drawing out talent and skills far beyond what even our children believe possible. Like coaches, parents are role models to kids, showing them the way of excellence more through our lives than through our words. One of the most successful college basketball coaches of all time, John Wooden, shares this advice with parents: "Be slow to criticize and quick to commend. Being a role model is the most powerful form of educating. Youngsters need good models more than they need critics. It's one of a parent's greatest responsibilities and opportunities. The person you are is the person your child will become."[32]

Understanding the power of coaching for developing character, Benedict recommends enlisting people to help train members of the family team, telling us to choose them *for their good repute . . . virtuous living and wise teaching* (RB, 21). My wife and I are indebted to dozens of coaches, both men and women, for the positive influence they've had on our kids. Benedict encourages us to ask for assistance in training the members of our family. He also recommends *mature and wise brothers [or sisters]* who come alongside struggling family members to offer support and strength *lest [they] be overwhelmed by excessive sorrow* (RB, 27).

As parents, we are wise to enlist the support of mature people to help us train our children. These family "coaches" may include relatives, teachers, athletic coaches, music or dance instructors, counselors, friends of the family, or wise people from the community of faith. We've been blessed with many such "coaches" who have supported us in stretching and strengthening our kids. In the *Exercises* section at the end of this chapter, I've adapted Benedict's wisdom on leadership, offering coaching tips for parents as we press on in training our children with excellence on the family team.

Rules of the Game

All team sports have rules and all athletes occasionally break those rules. Referees or umpires sort out these infractions. Most sports have different penalties for different degrees of violations. Take soccer for example:

any unsportsmanlike conduct elicits a verbal warning
from the referee. A more serious infraction stops the
play and gives a free kick to the other team. A foul that
jeopardizes the players' safety or flouts the rules draws
a yellow card and sends the offender out of the game
to sit on the bench for a time. The most flagrant type
of violation in soccer is met with a red card, a penalty
that ejects a player from the game.

In a similar manner, there are times in every family
when parents become referees and must deal with violations of family rules. After warnings and lesser forms of
penalties are found to be ineffective we must take further steps. Those children who insist on living in their
own world without regard to the greater life of the family and the shared rules of the home may need to be
sent to the "bench" for a time. Benedict is very clear
on the need for such referee action in the monastic family: *Those guilty of a serious fault are to be excluded from
both the table and the oratory* (RB, 25). In our home, as
in others, this penalty has been called "time out." Such
removal from the playing field may simply mean being
sent to a room or a "time out" chair. Time out may
also mean exclusion from family activities or removal
of privileges. Acting as referee or umpire, a parent provides boundaries and protection for the whole family as
they enforce the rules of the family.

Parents determine the length of the penalty, and also
how to get that family member back in the game once
the penalty time is up. Through these time outs, children gain a new perspective on life. Sometimes they
will experience a shift that allows them to play better

and be a better teammate. In Maurice Sendak's story, *Where the Wild Things Are,* though Max was sent to his room for wild behavior, he eventually grew tired of mischievous exploits in the far reaches of his imagination "and wanted to be where someone loved him best of all." He wanted to come back home. Children feel an inner longing to be where someone loves them best of all.

In some cases, though, even after parental warnings, removal of privileges and time outs, some children insist upon their own way at the expense of the rest of the family. When children continue to reject parental guidance, we lie awake at night wondering where we went wrong and what we now must do. My wife and I have labored at times over difficult decisions concerning the behaviors and attitudes of our children.

Benedict tells us to act wisely, not harshly, in such times. We have often prayed for our children in the midst of their difficulties, so that God, as Benedict reminds us, *who can do all things, may bring about the health of the sick one* (RB, 28). However, if every effort seems to fall short of reaching a wild child, a parent may need to pull out a "red card" and remove a child from normal play for a longer period of time. In order to protect the rest of the family and also to care for the unique needs of a difficult child, we may need to remove a child from the family for a longer period of time.

Practically speaking, such extraordinary measures will be for teenagers who by their actions threaten to break apart the family. We only remove a child from the home when the following support systems are in place: alternate housing for the child; a professional counselor enlisted for family therapy; and several adult friends who know you and your child well. These trusted persons continue to offer love and support to the child in difficulty, regardless of the response from the child.

Even in the face of "red card" type penalties, we continue to love our wild child and pray for his or her return and restoration. Welcome your children home as soon as possible, when their hearts are willing to rejoin the family and live as members of the family "team." The family is intended to be a place of love and spiritual growth, not a juvenile court of law. The only reason we blow the whistle is to get our kids back on the field as soon as possible to enjoy the sport they love most, that of growing up as part of a loving team called family.

Team Training

Every healthy family has problems. Every troubled family has strengths. As members of a family team, we all participate in training, seeking to strengthen one another in body and soul, utilizing a wide variety of exercises. Health in the home has its roots in the health of the parents. How can we raise spiritually healthy children unless we attend to our own spiritual health and growth? Children need more than "Do as I say not as I do." They need wise adults who will nurture them through intentional, long-term training and love.

We do not need to burden ourselves with unrealistic parenting expectations. All parents make mistakes. Without trying, we inevitably hand children both good gifts and troubles. As children, we received both health and sickness from our parents. Our parents received the same from their parents. As parents, we need to take responsibility for our own healing and do all we can to avoid passing the problems we received from our parents or grandparents to our children. We have little control over what we received from our parents when we were children. As parents, we have some choice over what we will pass on to our children.

When someone breaks the rules, we seek to train him or her in love. Such training stretches and strengthens the family body and soul. With more severe infractions, healing sometimes is neither quick nor comfortable. Athletes who break a bone or tear a ligament may be out for a season, but with proper resetting by a professional and time for healing, they will be able to return to the game they love.

One of the most loved qualities of Benedict's *Rule* is his moderate voice. Benedict loves to state rules, and then offer gentle exceptions. *If any community members, following their own ways, leave the monastery but then wish to return, they must first promise to make full amends for leaving. Let them be received back. . . . If they leave again, or even a third time, they should be readmitted under the same conditions* (RB, 29). Just as broken bones heal even stronger than the original, even so, broken families can also find healing and restoration over time with God's help.

In this chapter, we have looked at a variety of approaches to training within the family. Just as important as training in sports, music, theater or dance, family training helps mature our children by increasing their capacity for love. The restoration and ongoing training of family members is one of the most important works of family spirituality. Parents have a wide variety of options for this training, including patterns from our own childhood, wisdom from friends around us, and guidance found in books, including the Bible. Through the exercise of family training, we stretch and strengthen our children to go out into this world as grown adults, ready to build up others in the way of love.

FAMILY TRAINING EXERCISES

EXERCISE 1: Coaching Tips

The following list of ten "coaching tips" comes from chapter 64 of the *Rule*. Benedict writes of the qualities for spiritual leadership in the monastery. I've adapted them for coaching and training our children in the home. Circle one or two of these to put into practice on your family playing field this month.

1. Strive for goodness of life and wisdom in the way we teach and train our children. Our goal must be to seek the best interest of our children, not our own personal advancement.

2. Fill our lives with a treasury of knowledge from which we can "bring out what is new and what is

old."[33] We are wise to spend time understanding wisdom found in Scripture.

3. Be temperate and merciful, always letting "mercy triumph over judgment,"[34] so that we too may be filled with mercy.

4. Hate faults but love family members. In all aspects of family training, use moderation and avoid extremes.

5. Beware of rubbing too hard to remove the rust, or we may break the vessel. Learn to distrust our own frail nature and remember "not to crush the bruised reed nor snuff out the smoldering wick."

6. Prune away faults on the team with wisdom and love as we see best for each individual member.

7. Strive to be loved more than feared, showing forethought and consideration in the responsibilities we give to our children.

8. Be discerning and moderate in assigning tasks to members of the family team, drawing upon examples of wisdom and discretion from the Bible and also the examples of wise people we know.

9. Arrange everything so the strong have something to yearn for and the weak nothing to run from.

10. Live what we teach, practice what we preach, and walk what we talk.

EXERCISE 2: Yellow Cards and Penalty Boxes

In soccer, a referee blows a whistle when there is a violation of the rules. Sometimes, a player receives a "yellow card" and must go to the bench. In the same manner, there comes a time in all homes when parents need to blow the whistle and help a child take "time out" from the action. This exercise is for parents who have struggled with training in the home. Children want to be treated fairly, and have an inner sense of fair play. Try a sporting and playful approach to "time out" in your home by handing out yellow cards or creating your own family "penalty box."

- Warn the child of behaviors or attitudes that may warrant a time out. These warnings are best heard by a child when they are spoken in a playful or encouraging tone rather than a nagging voice.

- After sufficient warnings and no change in attitude or behavior, "blow the whistle," hand out a yellow card and remove the child to a time out place.

- Choose a place in the house as the location for the "Bench" or "Penalty Box." This place should be easily viewable by parents, yet free from distractions and diversions for children.

- Remove other tempting activities (remote control to the TV, music, books, comics, and toys) that might distract the player from getting back into the game.

- Decide on the appropriate penalty period, and give the child a clear notice that the timer has begun. We've used an egg timer, setting the penalty clock to tick away and "ding" when time is up. If your child chooses to go back out "into the game" before the time is up, send him back to the bench or penalty box with a warning and add a little time to the penalty.

* Expect that the behavior or attitude problem will change. If it hasn't, assign more time out or alter the form of training to better help the child adjust their behavior.

* For some more serious fouls, the time in the box may include missing important family events such as family game time, time at a computer, turning off the television, or missing a family outing.

* For teenage children, the "bench" or "penalty box" might include withheld privileges, no access to the family car, staying home rather than spending time at a friend's house, or missing a sporting event.

* At the end of the penalty time, have a "coach to player" talk about the rules of the game and fair play, and then send your child back out to play with excellence.

EXERCISE 3: Parenting Care

Not all harmful behaviors and attitudes belong to children in the family. As parents, we have our own problems in our behavior and attitudes. Some of these may be dealt with best by taking parenting "time out." Grown-up forms of time out may include the following:

* Stepping away from a difficult situation with children when our anger has pushed into the red zone. We are wise to ask another adult to step in at times and help

us when we become unable to parent with fairness, love, and wisdom.

♦ Confess hurtful behaviors or attitudes to a wise person.

♦ Enter into counseling to deal with pent-up emotions or unresolved inner struggles.

♦ Go away on a retreat for discernment. Seek out guidance from a wise friend, counselor, pastor, or spiritual director.

♦ Check into a treatment center to deal with an addiction problem.

♦ Join a small group or a 12–step program for support and accountability.

♦ Is there currently a need for "time out" in your life? If so, what form will this time take?

EXERCISE 4: Seed Time

A single mom I know deals with training in the home through activities she calls "Seed Time." This mom knows what most gardeners know: that some of the finest lessons a person can learn are discovered in the garden. Here then are a few activities for Seed Time, positive ways to nurture a child needing the training lessons from the garden of the soul.

Ten Seed Time activities

1. When a child is misbehaving, try taking a walk outside together to observe growing things: look at plants, trees, flowers, or a forest. Try collecting

similar items on each of these walks: leaves, rocks, flowers, seeds.

2. When a child is having a temper tantrum, offer to climb a tree together to sit still and listen to the wind.

3. For an alternative form of time out, play catch with a baseball and mitts, or pass a soccer ball together.

4. Garden together: always keep some bulbs or seeds on hand for planting at various times of the year.

5. Pull weeds together in a flowerbed.

6. Spread some mulch, or a bag of topsoil, as ground cover in flowerbeds.

7. Browse a book of artwork or a color photo magazine like *National Geographic* together. Get out scissors, paper and glue, and make a collage of favorite photos from the magazine.

8. To deal with a destructive attitude in a child, build something together. Get out a box of Legos, K'nex, Erector Set, or model car to build. Work on building this project only during Seed Time.

9. Water the plants in the house or the flowerbeds outside.

10. As an alternative form of "penalty," surprise your child, and offer to bake cookies together, encouraging your child to do much of the measuring, mixing, shaping, and spatula work.

EXERCISE 5: Coaching Inventory

* Assess your approach to training using the Benedictine principles. All these are taken from chapter 27 of the *Rule*. For each item, write out your comment or evaluation of your approach to strengthening the family in light of Benedict's principles.

* A parent *must exercise the utmost care and concern for the wayward because, "it is not the healthy who need a physician, but the sick"* (Matt. 9:12).

* A parent *ought to use every skill of a wise physician . . . support the wavering sister or brother, urge them to be humble as a way of making satisfaction.*

* After disciplining a child, a parent should *console them lest they be overwhelmed by excessive sorrow.*

* Training is an expression of a parent's love, *as the apostle also says, "Let love be reaffirmed."*

* Parents are wise to *pray for the one* being disciplined.

* It is the parent's responsibility *to have great concern and to act with all speed, discernment, and diligence in order not to lose any of the sheep entrusted to them.*

* Parents should realize *that they have undertaken care of the sick, not tyranny over the healthy.*

* Parents are to build up children and offer themselves in service to their children. Like a shepherd, a parent's calling is to *strengthen the weak . . . heal the sick . . . bind up the injured . . . bring back the strays . . . search for the lost* (Ezekiel 34:2–4).

- Parents are wise to *imitate the loving example of Christ, the Good Shepherd, who left the ninety-nine sheep in the mountains and went in search for the one sheep that had strayed.*

- Parents offer compassion to children through training and take great care to restore children fully after a time of penalty on the sidelines. *So great was Christ's compassion for its weakness that "he mercifully placed it on his sacred shoulders" and so carried it back to the flock* (Luke 15:5).

EXERCISE 6: Building Character on the Family Team

What are the methods for offering our children positive, loving training in the home? When discipline is viewed as merely "punishing offenders for breaking the law," parental discipline will not be very effective in building lasting character in our children. When we view discipline from a spiritual perspective, this aspect of parenting becomes like athletic training. The following steps of discipline are drawn from the *Rule,* chapter 28.

1. *Verbal Training:*

   - *The ointment of encouragement:* We are wise to pay attention to this insight of Benedict, that encouragement is a form of the disciplined life together.

   - *Frequent reproof for faults:* The attitude offered while speaking corrections to children helps it to be received. Positive attitudes in the speaker tend to generate more willing reception by the listener.

2. *Spiritual Training:*

- *The medicine of Scripture:* the Bible is described as "living and active, sharper than any double-edged sword, penetrating even to dividing soul and spirit . . . judging the thoughts and attitudes of the heart."[35] We are wise to employ such an effective tool of training by encouraging our children to read, study, memorize and meditate upon wisdom from the Bible.

- *All the members should pray for them so that God, who can do all things, may bring about the health of the sick one.* Through prayer we approach God to "receive mercy and find help in our time of need."[36] Prayer offers a family a shared heart activity, centering our lives upon the love of God poured out into our hearts.

3. *Training the Body:*

- *Applying the compresses:* Benedict refers to limiting a person's privileges or putting a squeeze on a family member's freedom. This form of training is especially powerful in the teenage years, when personal freedoms are so highly valued and the price tag of responsibility so easily disregarded.

- *The cauterizing iron of excommunication:* Though the word "excommunication" sounds punitive and excessive, as Benedict used this word, is simply refers to what parents call time out, removal to the "bench" or "penalty box" for a set amount of time.

+ Benedict also mentions other forms of physical training, including fasting (removal of food), silence (removal of speech) and solitude (removal from people) as approaches to learning our place within the family. Spiritual disciplines that train the body can help bring healing and growth in our children.

EXERCISE 7: Playful Parenting

Lawrence J. Cohen, Ph.D., offers delightful alternative forms of discipline in his book *Playful Parenting* (New York: Ballantine Books, 2001). In his chapter "Rethink the Way We Discipline," he introduces what he calls "a fresh look at discipline" (see pages 232–252). Try one of these ideas in your family this week.

+ *Cool off:* Rather than jumping into a disciplinary problem in the heat of the moment, take a little time to settle down, cool off and respond wisely rather than react rashly. "Talking to other parents is one of the best ways to cool off," writes Cohen.

+ *Make a connection:* Look into your child's eyes to connect with their soul and seek the reason behind the outer actions. Cohen even suggests "a hug, some quiet time together, wrestling or running around outside the house, a snack, or a talk."

- *Choose a "Meeting on the Couch" over a "Time out":* Agree with your child that either parent or child can call a meeting on the couch if there is a problem. The other person must show up for a meeting when it is called. "Try to stay on the couch until both of you are ready to go back and do things differently from before," offers Cohen.

- *Play!* Rather than threaten, yell or nag, why not play with your child as a creative alternative to discipline. "In the rush to punish children" reminds Cohen, "we forget that the essence of discipline is to *teach.*"

- *Instill good judgment and look underneath the surface:* Children need more than mere punishment: they need help growing up. When parents take time to look behind the actions, we may see what is holding them back.

- *Prevent instead of punish:* According to Cohen, "The more playtime you have with your children, especially play where they get to be in charge and you help them maintain their closeness and confidence, the less you will need any of these alternatives to punishment."

- *Know your child and set clear limits:* Finally, Cohen suggests that each child is unique and responds to situations in their own unique ways. Benedict understood this as well. Speaking of the father figure in the monastery, Benedict wrote, *He must so arrange everything that the strong have something to yearn for and the weak nothing to run from* (RB, 64).

❧ Chapter Four ❧

Gather in the Kitchen

Recipes for a Healthy Lifestyle

*I was hungry and you gave me something to eat, I
was thirsty and you gave me something to drink.*
— Matthew 25:35

In our home, the kitchen is more than just a place where
we prepare meals. Our kitchen is a gathering place for
family and friends. When we built our home ten years
ago, we spent a lot of time considering the floor plan for
the kitchen and dining room. We built a large room filled
with light and laughter, sugar and spice, intimacy and
hospitality. Like a well-planned kitchen, family spirituality provides a place for nurturing health and growth in
the family. Family health is nourished when members of
the family care for one another and support others even
in their weaknesses. Family health doesn't happen by
chance, but rather develops from healthy habits the family learns together. In this chapter we will look together
at down-to-earth spiritual approaches to family health.
Like recipes in cookbooks, these ideas only nourish the
family when opened and put into practice.

Feeding the Family

I believe the task of feeding the family encompasses a lot more than merely putting food on the table. Food is an expression of love. Mealtimes are a daily opportunity to nourish the soul of the family. In our home, we begin every meal by joining hands in a circle and offering a short prayer or song of thanks to God. As Sarah McElwain writes in *Saying Grace: Blessings for the Family Table,* "Expressing gratitude for the food on our tables is universal. People in all times and in every place have felt the need to say thanks for what they are about to eat."[37]

The roots of the Jewish and Christian faith center upon the sacred act of eating together. One of the holiest days of the Jewish year focuses upon a sacred meal, Passover, in which Jewish families eat the Passover together in remembrance of the holy history of the exodus of Israel from bondage in Egypt. As a Jew, Jesus loved sharing meals with people. He loved being with people at mealtimes and described eternal life as a great banquet feast. On the night before he was killed, he broke bread and shared a common cup together with his closest friends, a meal that has become one of the central acts of the Christian faith — the Lord's Supper or Eucharist.

One of my favorite stories of Jesus at mealtime, though, comes from the Gospel of Luke, in the account of Jesus at Emmaus.[38] In this story, two mourners are returning home, traveling seven miles on foot to their village. They have witnessed the death of Jesus but know nothing of his resurrection. As they walk, a stranger joins them and walks with them. After several hours of conversing together along the road, they arrive at their village and welcome the stranger into their home for the night. The stranger takes bread, gives thanks, breaks it, and shares it with them. It is at that moment at table together that they recognize the stranger to be Jesus. Their hearts are filled with a newly found hope and joy as they hurry back to Jerusalem to tell others their story, "how Jesus was recognized by them when he broke the bread."[39]

One of the chief ways we recognize the presence of God is when we give thanks and break bread together at our family table. Eating together provides an opportunity to clearly see the blessings in our midst. If we develop the habit of giving thanks for our food, we cultivate the ability to appreciate the many gifts that sustain and support our bodies and souls. In a society where materialism and marketing prod children to want more and more, taking a moment to say grace helps them see how much they already have.

In his down-to-earth wisdom Benedict offers guidance for the daily work of feeding the monastic family. He begins with the character qualifications of the person assigned to oversee food service in the monastery, a person Benedict called the cellarer:

As cellarer of the monastery, there should be chosen from the community someone who is wise, mature in conduct, temperate, not an excessive eater, not proud, excitable, offensive, dilatory or wasteful, but God-fearing. . . . They must show every care and concern for the sick, children, guests and the poor. . . . They should not be prone to greed, nor be wasteful and extravagant with the goods of the monastery. . . . They will provide the members their allotted amount of food without any pride or delay. (RB, 31)

As food providers in our home, we might chew upon the wisdom of Benedict. Benedict wrote that monks *should each try to be the first to show respect to the other, supporting with the greatest patience one another's weaknesses of body or behavior* (RB, 72). Benedict focused attention upon each member of the community caring for one another in body, mind, and spirit. He refused to allow the body to be demeaned for the sake of the spirit.

Today, Benedict would encourage parents to strive for wisdom, maturity in our conduct, temperance and moderation in our words and actions, care and concern for the needy, as well as developing a lifestyle of generosity, resourcefulness and simplicity. We feed the family as much by what fills our spirit as we do by what fills our bowls and platters. In the home, mealtimes signify more than mere consumption of food for bodily nourishment. They are times in which the family gathers to enjoy God's presence discovered as we give thanks, break bread, and share life together.

Menu Choices

Often when I cook, I look through the kitchen to see what options are available. Though we have plenty of great cookbooks, I also enjoy the creative challenge of pulling various items out of the fridge and pantry, and seeing what I can cook up from what's on hand. This work in the kitchen involves the art of discernment: looking over the options, choosing some, leaving some, and then creatively putting together the menu that will best feed the family. Like learning to cook, discernment is a highly valuable skill to develop in the family. Every child is different, requiring different approaches to parenting.

As Benedict affirms, *Every age and level of understanding should receive appropriate treatment* (RB, 30). In this instruction Benedict calls parents to practice the art of discernment. Not every choice is the best choice for the family. Time, space, energy, finances, and resources are limited. Choices must be made. If parents fail to make choices for the family, choices will invariably come upon the family through circumstances, passions, and fads. These unchosen choices are often less desirable for the overall growth of the family than choices made with discernment and intention.

Opportunities arise every day to exercise discernment, asking us to separate what is appropriate from what is inappropriate, and what is healthy from what is unhealthy. I recently had a dad ask me if I thought an award-winning movie on slum life was appropriate for their teenage children. I gave him my opinion and commended him for weighing out this choice for his family. When we exercise discernment on behalf of our children we try to be mindful of their temperament and age, as well as their gifts and weaknesses. I believe that no single approach to parenting will work for every child. In all things, we seek to choose what is best for each individual member of the family, as well as what will benefit the family as a whole. Every child is different. Every season of parenting is different. There are no cookie-cutter molds in raising a healthy family.

Living Simply

A life of simplicity is best learned by example. One aspect of family life involves what we eat and what we wear. We do not need rooms full of clothing or refrigerators full of food to be happy. When monks enter the monastery, they voluntarily give up their possessions and enter a life of simplicity, focused upon loving God and loving others. Living simply invites us to see all life as a gift from God. Within a healthy family, the role of gratitude gets center stage. As gratitude takes her place within the family, every cast member begins to see objects as gifts to be shared, not as private possessions to be hoarded. When gratitude takes center stage in a home, we discover anew the delight of living simply and find pleasure in sharing God's good gifts with others. Simplicity in family life may include giving away what we do not use or need to help those who cannot afford such items.

Like most middle-class families, our family has more stuff than we need. Of course, children will complain about clothes. That's part of acting as a child. Benedict faced the same problem in his day. *Monastics must not*

complain about the color or coarseness of all these arti-
cles. Whenever new clothing is received, the old should be
returned at once and stored in a wardrobe for the poor
(RB, 55). When children complain, we are wise to refo-
cus them upon the things of the heart. When kids whine
about clothes, gently remind them that clothes, like all
our possessions, are gifts given to us for our well being.
We encouraged our children to choose what they want
to wear, but always reserved the right to veto their
choice if it seemed inappropriate for the occasion. We've
also sorted through our children's clothes and shoes to
take non-worn items to the thrift store. We are wise to
teach children to care for their possessions, including
training children to help with the laundry. This is much
easier to write about than to carry out. How often did
we hear our children say, "I can't find any clean socks
or underwear"?

Children learn best, not through nagging, but through
playful actions. Everyone is expected to share in the care
of possessions. As parents, we train our children to care
for the world by caring for their belongings and for
one another. As the Book of Acts describes the earliest
Christians, "All the believers were one in heart and mind.
No one claimed that any of his possessions was his own,
but they shared everything they had."[40] Our world is
starved for love. Mother Teresa once wrote:

> I think the world today is upside down, and is
> suffering so much, because there is so very little
> love in the homes and in family life. We have no
> time for our children, we have no time for each

other; there is no time to enjoy each other. Love begins at home; love lives in homes.[41]

As parents, when we invest time in our children, especially "to enjoy each other," our children learn to live a life of love, a life filled with acts of kindness and compassion, especially for those in need. As Benedict teaches, *"Distribution was made as each had need" (Acts 4:35). By this we do not imply that there should be favoritism . . . but rather consideration for weaknesses* (RB, 34). When we've begun to live in simplicity within our family life, we learn to relax and be ourselves, without having to role-play or pretend. We learn to live simply with love, gratitude, and contentment. In so doing we will have sufficient means to share with others out of the abundance of our hearts. As Gandhi taught, "Live simply that others may simply live."

Caring for Others

The home is the first place we learn to care for others, including caring for the body, mind, and spirit. After we've provided the best care possible for our family members and made our best assessment of the health care needs in our home, we call the doctor and make an appointment when further care is needed. Benedict clearly affirmed caring for the physical needs of the members of his monastic family. He planned the monastic home to include a care center, an infirmary, and instructed monks to care for those who are suffering from an illness. *Care of the sick must rank above and before all else so that they may truly be served as Christ. . . . Let a separate room be designated for the sick, and let them be served by an attendant who is God-fearing, attentive and concerned* (RB, 36).

When our children are not well, as parents we become especially responsive to their needs, looking for the best ways to restore health. I remember lying in a sick bay as a child, suffering from bronchitis, and breathing steam from the vaporizer. For all the efforts taken to bring about my cure, it was my mom's reassuring voice that brought me the greatest comfort. Benedict councils us to be deeply concerned about those who are not well and to treat them with attentive warmth and love.

Caring for the sick can happen in many different ways, including a card offering encouragement, a home-cooked meal, a compassionate presence or a listening ear. Through compassion we suffer with the sick, bearing their burden. Through attentive listening we discern the nature of the sickness and seek the best help available. When our second son, Stefan, was in middle school, he was chosen to serve as a peer counselor at his school. Stefan described how this program had helped him become a better listener. "I was taught how to reach out to people. When you see somebody crying, you don't just say, 'Oh, there's someone crying.' You go to them and ask, 'What's wrong?' Then you take time to listen. When you listen, you can really help people through their problems."

In homes, the youngest and the oldest also have special needs, requiring special care. Benedict offers practical guidance regarding care for the elderly and the young. *Respect the elders and love the young. . . . Since their lack of strength must always be taken into account, they should certainly not be required to follow the strictness of the rule with regard to food, but should be treated with kindly consideration* (RB, 4 and 37). As a family, we seek ways to practice the art of kindness toward the old and young. Here are a few such ideas:

- Beyond the walls of our home, we are wise to take our children to visit the elderly, modeling the care we hope to receive when we turn ninety. A foundation well laid in childhood will offer a lifetime of care, bringing help to many.

- We may also offer to help care for children in another family through babysitting, mentoring, tutoring, car-pooling, and other types of care.

- We can reach out to relatives and friends who are ill and drop off a meal or offer to pick up groceries for homebound neighbors.

In the journey of our lives from childhood to old age, parents and children alike need the help of others. Within the family, we hope to create a loving environment of care and compassion that will support each member in their time of need, as well as bring such care and compassion to our community and world.

The Sacred Heart of Sexuality

While traveling in Europe as a college student, I spent a week in Paris. During this week, I visited the Sacré

Coeur basilica, the church of the "sacred heart." As I stepped off the Paris Metro and took the escalator up to the street level, the basilica was nowhere in sight. Instead, my eyes were confronted by sex for sale. I had entered the Parisian red light district and was taken off guard. In the midst of all the sex shops, I kept looking for the Sacred Heart basilica. At last I glimpsed the church up a side street. There she sat high on a hill overlooking the city. After climbing several hundred steps, I was out of breath as I entered that basilica. Stepping inside the Sacré Coeur, my breath was taken away again by the beauty of that place. Over the front altar, in a grand mosaic, Christ reached out with extended arms to welcome people home.

Later, I realized the parable that experience provided concerning our sexuality. We emerge from childhood seeking what is beautiful and good. In our teenage years, we head up into adulthood, and come face to face with sexual choices. At that crossroad, we have hard choices to make concerning our sexuality. Two equally harmful options are offered along the way: either we indulge our sexual nature in the empty hope that life fulfillment is found in gratifying our bodily desires. Or, we deny our sexual nature as corrupt, believing that sex is bad. The middle way is the way into the "sacred heart" of our sexual selves.

This middle way affirms sex as a gift from God to be enjoyed. We do not focus upon the pornography and perversity offered to us because the eyes of our hearts are set upon the higher beauty of sex that reflects the most intimate and loving aspects of ourselves. Eventually, we come into the sanctuary of a loving relationship and allow ourselves to be embraced and welcomed by the sacred heart of God.

The family is vital to a person's spiritual and sexual growth. In a healthy family, sexuality is discovered within the enclosure of love, not out in the street among strangers. Monks live their sexual lives within the protection of God's gift of celibacy. As parents, we live our sexual lives within the protection of marriage. Our children live their sexual lives within the protection of singleness.

These protective enclosures are gifts provided for our good. Within these walls we grow in wholeness and love. Wise parents instruct children about their sexuality as a beautiful part of their lives with God. Too many parents avoid the subject of sex with their children, out of embarrassment or ignorance. When we neglect to talk with our children about sex, we are not helping them climb the stairs to the Sacré Coeur. We need to guide them to an understanding of this precious part of themselves. When we give our children a sense of their sexuality as a holy gift to be cherished, they will learn to value and protect this gift, so that sexuality emerges into a right and pleasing place in their lives.

Fasting and Feasting

Every night the family fasts. Every morning the family breaks the fast with the first meal of the day, "breakfast." The family is wise to set aside times for both fasting and feasting and to devote space in the family schedule for these two healthy habits. As a spiritual practice, fasting is practiced by Jews, Christians, and Muslims the world around. Benedict understood fasting as an essential spiritual habit. *In other words, let each one deny themselves some food, drink, sleep, needless talking and idle jesting, and look forward to holy Easter with joy and spiritual longing* (RB, 49). Fasting wakes up our spiritual longing. In turning away for a time from bodily pleasures, we turn our lives toward what is truly healthy for us in body and soul.

Though fasting may be practiced at various times through the year, many people choose a specific way to fast during the forty days of Lent in the spring. Fasting is more than merely giving up a meal or a type of food or drink. It is opening up our lives to God and compassionately reaching out to needy people with practical acts of kindness.

Fasting is intended to untie invisible cords that keep us from a life of love and to free us from all forms of addiction and unhealthy bondage. Children can be taught to fast. Talk together in the home about specific ways to practice fasting as a family. In a home of abundance, fasting unites us with a world in need. Read together about people in the world who are suffering. Get out a globe or map of the world and study the situations of people from other nations who are in need. As you fast, offer prayers for those in need, asking God to give you and your children a heart of compassion. When the fast is completed, break your fast with a simple meal, giving thanks to God for the gift of life.

The ancient spiritual practice of fasting is balanced by feasting and enjoying special celebration days. Find many reasons to celebrate, because children love parties. Birthdays, anniversaries, and holidays, as well as great life events such as births, graduations, weddings, retirements, and even deaths, are important occasions to gather and express our joy and gratitude for the many gifts in our lives. Roll out the streamers, blow up balloons, bring out special tablecloths and banners, make tasty foods, dance and sing together as you fill your home with the joyous spirit of celebration. As families learn to fast and feast, a spirit of compassion and generosity will grow in the home, freeing us to give of our lives to help others in need. As Isaiah promises, "If you spend yourselves in behalf of the hungry and satisfy the needs of the oppressed, then your light will rise in the darkness, and your night will become like the noonday. . . . You will be like a well-watered garden, like a spring whose waters never fail."[42]

Bread for the World

We live in a hungry world. We do not need to travel very far before we bump into hungry people. Though I live in a beautiful resort town on the Oregon coast, featuring the highest property values in the state, there are many hungry families living in our village. Recently, concerned citizens of our city formed a food pantry to meet this need. Supported by citizen volunteers, local churches, as well as the county and state food bank, this food pantry now helps families feed their children every week when financial resources have been depleted.

Every Benedictine monastery also cares for the needy in a variety of ways. In Benedict's time, the world also faced overwhelming needs, including famine, drought, invasion by foreign military powers, and extreme poverty. In such a world of need, Benedict always bore in mind *what is said in the Acts of the Apostles: 'Distribution was made to each one as he had need'* (RB, 55). Monasteries have always welcomed the poor and the needy. Benedictine monks are committed to a life of prayer, manual labor and voluntary poverty, enabling them to produce more than they need, and thus have an abundance to give away to needy people in the world around them. I was once told by a Benedictine monk that monks work twenty-four hours per week and are able to produce enough to provide for their needs and give to the needy in the community.

How can families reach out to the needy in their community and in the world? As a family, we have opportunities to help disadvantaged families in our community as well as sponsoring children in developing countries suffering from illness and starvation. We can send letters, packages of gifts, financial support, and of course can offer our prayers. Out of the comfort we have received, "we can comfort those in any trouble with the comfort we ourselves have received from God."[43]

There are many great charitable organizations that provide good avenues for families to help others around the world. Look into international relief organizations that are offering aid to the world's neediest people:

- Bread for the World: *www.bread.org;*

- Compassion International: *www.compassion.com;*

- Samaritan's Purse: *www.samaritanspurse.org;*

- Heifer International: *www.heifer.org;*

- Habitat for Humanity: *www.habitat.org;*

- Catholic Relief Services: *http://crs.org;*

- World Relief: *www.worldrelief.org;*

- World Vision: *www.worldvision.org;*

- World Concern: *www.worldconcern.org.*

One family activity may include accessing the web-site of one of these groups or writing off for a packet of information from them. Help your children explore the needs of the world and how organizations are bringing help and hope to needy people. Then, at a family meeting, agree upon a specific way to help others. This may involve a weekly habit, a seasonal activity or an annual project in your family. In the *Exercises* section below, there are more ideas for family involvement in helping to provide daily bread to hungry people around the world. One of the greatest gifts we can give our children is the confidence that they can make a difference for good in this world by giving their lives away to help others in need.

FAMILY HEALTH EXERCISES

EXERCISE 1: Family Mealtimes

Here are five principles for mealtimes together. As a
family, decide how many family meals you will commit to sharing each week. If you currently only eat two
meals together per week, try adding several more. At
these meals, seek to implement one or more of these
principles.

1. *Build up the family through meals. Show every
    care and concern for the sick, young, guests and the
    poor* (RB, 31). So Benedict writes of mealtime. The
    family is a place of mutual service and love, even
    in the basic tasks of food preparation. Benedict
    warns the cook not to annoy family members,
    knowing how much power resides in the person
    in charge of food. The attitude in which a meal is
    served is as important for family nutrition as what
    is being served. As the Book of Proverbs confirms,
    "Better a dry crust with peace and quiet than a
    house full of feasting with strife."[44]

2. *Include the whole family in meal preparation and
    cleanup.* Benedict encourages the enlistment of
    kitchen helpers, *that with assistance it becomes
    possible to perform the duties of the office calmly*
    (RB, 31). Try to involve all family members in meal
    preparation through the week. We've used a simple
    homemade chore chart agreed upon by the whole
    family, giving order to mealtime preparation and

cleanup. One of the basic skills children need to learn before becoming adults is meal preparation.

3. *Eat simply.* According to Benedict, the person making meals *should not be prone to greed, not be wasteful and extravagant with the goods of the monastery, but should do everything with moderation* (RB, 31). Benedict would warn us today from buying faddish foods, fast foods, or overly preprocessed foods. Instead, Benedict would focus upon wholesome foods, natural products, locally grown produce and simple menus. One home-cooked meal satisfies a family more than ten meals out. Restaurant meals make for good special occasions and celebrations. As seasons allow, eat locally grown fruits and vegetables, especially those you've grown in your own garden.

4. *Eat meals together each week.* As I've talked with a wide variety of parents across the nation over the past ten years, I've discovered most families seldom eat together. A 2003 study published by The National Center on Addiction and Substance Abuse at Columbia University revealed that families who eat at least five dinners together per week had fewer incidents of measurable family troubles. In contrast, families who eat two dinners or less per week had significantly higher rates of measurable family problems.[45] One of the most important family habits to develop is regular mealtimes together. Try sitting together around the dinner table for a family meal. Join hands in a

circle and give thanks to God for the many gifts
of goodness you've received through the day.

5. *Nurture gratitude.* Like all creatures, we need food
   to survive. Benedict tells the food service manager
   in the monastery to *provide the brothers their*
   allotted amount of food (RB, 31). Yet, we do not
   live simply to eat. We live to love and be loved.
   Food is one practical expression of God's love for
   our lives. Encourage a heart of gladness in the
   home and children will learn to live with grateful
   hearts for all God's good gifts. Benedict declared
   all utensils and goods of the monastery as sacred [as]
   vessels of the altar (RB, 31). Therefore, in all we do,
   including food preparation and kitchen chores,
   recognize God's presence and give thanks. The
   kitchen is set apart by God as a place of spiritual
   nourishment, and the dining room a place of
   beauty and abundance in family life together.

EXERCISE 2: Planting a Victory Garden

The size of the garden is not important. Think small.
We began with a 10'x10' garden in a borrowed corner
of a friend's backyard. Some other ideas for a Victory
Garden include a planter box on a sunny back porch, a
window ledge garden, or a flower pot garden. We took
up gardening early into our parenting years, partially
because we love fresh, home-grown fruits, herbs, flowers and vegetables on our table. But we've also learned
some great lessons together as a family through planting
a Victory Garden. Like much of life, gardening is learned

by trial and error. Here are some ideas that may be of help in starting a family tradition of a Victory Garden.

1. *Plan Your Victory Garden*

   - Begin early in the New Year, making a family plan to plant a Victory Garden.

   - Discuss together what types of things you would like to grow as a family.

   - Plan where your garden will be planted and even lay out a garden design.

2. *Prepare the Soil*

   - Depending upon your location and type of soil, the first step is soil preparation.

   - Rent or borrow a rotor-tiller and loosen the soil.

   - Add your own family compost to your garden soil.

   - Look in your local library or other resources about building your own compost bin.

   - Ask locals about soil conditions and natural additives for soil improvements.

3. *Collect What You Need*

   - Go shopping with your children, making it a Victory Garden expedition.

   - Buy seeds, seedlings, natural fertilizers, soil helpers, and anti-pest aids.

- Gather together all your gardening tools, buckets, gloves and stuff into one place in a shed or garage.

4. *Plant Seeds and Starts*

- Lay out the Victory Garden into plots or rows for various types of plants, vegetables, and flowers.

- Help your children plant seeds and seedlings into the soil.

- Use a hands-on approach to discover the wonder of seeds, roots, soil, and God's creation.

5. *Care for the Garden*

- Water your Victory Garden regularly.

- Weed the garden with your children.

- Thin out and tie up plants as needed.

- Try natural approaches to bug control.

6. *Harvest!*

- At last comes the day you've awaited for months: your first harvest!

- Out at your Victory Garden, celebrate your first harvest by offering a prayer of thanks to God for his goodness and for this good earth filled with growing things.

- Eat, enjoy and give away your harvest until the final plants produce their last fruit, flower, or vegetable.

* When October rolls around, it is time to prepare the garden for the winter, giving thanks to God for all the wonderful gifts and lessons you've learned from your Victory Garden.

EXERCISE 3: The Kitchen Chore Chart

Benedict assumed that all monks would have their turn helping out with kitchen tasks. *The members should serve one another. Consequently, no members will be excused from kitchen service . . . for such service increases reward and fosters love* (RB, 35). We used chore charts as a family to help us sort out who does what in the house and when these tasks get done. One chart was a calendar with each week of the year labeled with a letter: A, B, C, D through the year. Another chart was posted on the refrigerator, our Kitchen Chore Chart. We rotated Kitchen chores each week, according to the week: "A" week, "B" week, "C" week or "D" week. If you do not already have a schedule for family chores, try developing one this month. Here are a few samples:

DAILY KITCHEN CHORES

Week	Cook	Unload	Load	Clear/Clean
A	Oldest Son	Middle Son	Youngest Son	Dad
B	Dad	Oldest Son	Middle Son	Youngest Son
C	Youngest Son	Dad	Oldest Son	Middle Son
D	Middle Son	Youngest Son	Dad	Oldest Son

Along with kitchen chores, we ask our children to participate in daily and weekly chores. These tasks are chosen at a family meeting once or twice a year. Each household and age-level is different.

DAILY HOUSE CHORES

Oldest Son: make bed, sweep wood floor

Middle Son: make bed, take out trash

Youngest Son: make bed, care for dog

WEEKLY HOUSE CHORES (Saturday)

Oldest Son: sweep floors, clean living room, dust/oil woodwork, clean bedroom

Middle Son: shake rugs, sweep porch, bathe dog, clean bedroom, recycle

Youngest Son: vacuum carpets, wash car, clean bathroom, clean bedroom

EXERCISE 4: The Give-Away Game

The goods of the monastery, that is, its tools, clothing, or anything else, should be entrusted to members whom the prioress or abbot appoints and in whose manner of life they have confidence (RB, 32). Family spirituality calls people into a life of creative and compassionate service to others through giving of our lives and possessions. One creative way to enter into the spirit of giving is by playing the Give-Away Game. Before playing this game, at a family meeting, ask family members several questions:

- What pieces of clothing have I not worn for an entire year?

- What doesn't fit anymore?

* Which toys have stayed on the toy shelf too long?

* What in my room would make another little girl or boy happy to receive as a gift?

* What things do I really need and which ones don't I need anymore?

At the next family meeting, have everyone bring a particular material possession as a token for playing "The Give-Away Game."

Playing the give-away game

* Have each member of the family tell something they liked about one of their "give-away" treasures.

* Ask God to bless the people who will receive these belongings.

* Place all the items in boxes, and deliver them to a local thrift store, Goodwill, Salvation Army or other charitable organization that receives such donations.

EXERCISE 5: Needs & Wants Survey

Whoever needs less should thank God and not be distressed, but those who need more should feel humble because of their weakness (RB, 34). How are parents to discern between needs and wants in the family? Every family determines these boundaries uniquely. In this exercise, you'll find a set of statements for family discussion on needs and wants.

NEEDS AND WANTS SURVEY

Respond to each statement with one of the following evaluations:

Strongly Agree – Agree – Neutral – Disagree – Strongly Disagree

Then discuss your responses with one another.

1. We often discuss the difference between needs and wants.

2. Our family has all it needs.

3. Our family enjoys some luxuries.

4. Our family knows the difference between needs and wants.

5. We have studied Scripture together concerning material possessions and wealth.

6. The Bible has principles to teach us about needs and wants.

7. We are instructing our children about money, including giving, saving, and spending.

8. We have a family budget for giving, saving, and spending.

9. Our family enjoys giving to others.

10. We have local and national or international charitable organizations that we support.

11. We have seen poverty face to face and we know people who are poor.

12. We have taken regular steps towards simplifying our lifestyle.

13. We have read books on creative ways to live more simply.

14. We have served the needy in our community in some way.

15. Sometimes we feel the pinch of not having enough.

16. We have enough food, adequate shelter, clean drinking water, and basic medical care.

17. True poverty is the poverty we discover in our hearts before God.

18. True wealth is found in loving God and loving others, not in what we own.

19. We regularly spend quality time together as a family doing simple things together.

20. We know both how to fast and how to feast in our home.

EXERCISE 6: The Birds & the Bees

How do we educate our kids about sex? If we refuse to train our children about God's gift of sex, they will learn about this gift from others who may have a lesser view of the sacred heart of sexuality. Here are twelve practical ideas for talking about sex with your child.

Twelve ideas for talking with your child about sex

1. Take your children to wedding ceremonies and talk together about marriage vows. Tell your children about marriage, about living under marriage vows, and about God's gift of marriage.

2. Read and study the first two chapters of Genesis together as a family. With pre-school and early elementary age children, get a children's picture Bible for this time together.

3. Ask God to bring growth to your children, including physical development, intellectual understanding, emotional maturity and spiritual wisdom.

4. Teach your children correct names for male-female body parts, and use these names when talking about personal hygiene.

5. Help children to appreciate nature and the natural world, seeing all of creation, including our bodies, as expressions of God's creative goodness.

6. Discover "teachable moments" in which to talk with your children about sex and help your children discover more of God's beautiful design for sexuality.

7. Study nature together, including seeds, eggs, cells, fertilization, reproduction, birth, male and female differences in nature. Talk with your children about such elements in humans.

8. Study picture books together about bodies, physical development, how we are made. Go to the local library to check out books on the human body. Read them together with your children.

9. Offer simple, straightforward, age-appropriate answers to your children's questions about bodies, about sex, about where babies come from, about

birth. Get involved in your child's education at school when they are going over reproduction and sexuality. Review the materials handed out; use them to instruct your children about their own development.

10. Teach your children your morals and values about sex. We can't shield our children from all misinformation and corrosive influences with regard to sexuality. But a parent can help develop a child's moral character to grow into sexual maturity with innocence and integrity.

11. Provide your children with mature role models. Ask couples or individuals who are older and wiser than you to spend time with your children, to get to know them and invest in your family life. As parents, we are wise to help our children find spiritual fathers and mothers to help us raise our kids.

12. Be merciful with your children when they disappoint you and make mistakes. Forgive them, instruct them in wisdom, truth and grace and train them with compassion, mindful of your own failures and troubles, and always remember God's unfailing love.

EXERCISE 7: World Hunger Project

"Is not this the kind of fasting I have chosen: to loose the chains of injustice and untie the cords of the yoke, to set the oppressed free and break every yoke? Is it not to share your food with the hungry and to provide the poor wanderer with shelter?"[46] What can a family do to help when the problem of world hunger seems so overwhelming and often times so far away? Benedict would encourage us to build a bridge into needy people's lives through the spiritual habits of fasting and giving. Fasting not only purifies our lives and unites us closer to God, but also unites our lives with hungry people in the world and brings goodness back upon our homes and hearts. Giving not only helps those who receive but also brings joy to those who give. Try involving your family in a World Hunger Project. Here's how it works.

World Hunger Project

- Set aside a week for your World Hunger Project.
- Invite the family to fast. Instead of abstinence from food, offer the family a different kind of fast: abstinence from luxury activities or foods for a week. Here are a few possibilities: fast from watching television; stop playing electronic games; give up time on the computer and the Internet; write letters instead of calling people by phone; go without fast food or candy. All these things are luxuries in most parts of the world.
- During your World Hunger Project, focus instead upon alternative activities:

  - Enjoy family reading time together.
  - Watch a video available through a world hunger relief agency.
  - Study world hunger. Read stories of needy people in our world.

- Get out a globe or world map and learn about the geography of hunger.

- Write letters to elected officials expressing your concern about world hunger.

- Ask God to help those who suffer from hunger and malnutrition.

♦ Ask every family member to contribute towards the "World Hunger Fund." Send off a check to a hunger relief agency for world hunger relief.

♦ At the end of the "World Hunger" week, celebrate by eating a simple dinner of beans and rice.

♦ Offer thanks to God for the gift of life.

✤ Chapter Five ✤

Make Space, Give Time

Opening the Secrets
of Shared Life

How very good and pleasant it is when kindred live together in unity! —Psalm 133:1 (NRSV)

A common house design today includes a great room in which a variety of family activities take place, including entertainment, studies, play, reading, and listening to music. In our home, we have a great room that includes a wood stove, upright piano, a futon that doubles as a bed for overnight guests, a stereo, rocking chairs, original artwork hanging on the walls, as well as a bookshelf that contains a wide variety of books we've read aloud to our kids through the years. We've always tried to make our house a welcoming place where friends and guests can gather together and feel at home. Just as Margaret Wise Brown's classic children's book *Goodnight Moon* takes place "in the great green room," family life together grows in places where members of the family share time together. Fitting the lives of children and parents together into a harmonious whole takes wisdom and grace. Devoted families will work together over years to unite the stories of their lives into a beautiful book filled with tales of faith, hope, and love. In chapter five we'll open the pages of shared family life and explore ways to grow together as a family.

Family Schedules

On the wall in our dining room, we have a large bulletin board filled with schedules, lists, messages, and a calendar. At times in our family life you would have found sports schedules, camp dates, orthodontist appointments, school activities, work schedules, chore charts, and lists of things needing to be done around the house. Parents have the responsibility of managing the family schedule. Daily and weekly schedules are necessary in every family.

We are designed to live rhythmic lives. From the beginning, there have been times of light and darkness, morning and evening, work and rest, time alone and time together. The cycles of nature, including the movement of sun, moon, and stars, reveal the creative rhythms of life. Benedict offers wise principles for managing the creative rhythms of family life.

First, Benedict recommends bringing the family into a daily and weekly schedule. He writes, *It is the responsibility of the abbot to announce, day and night, the hour for the work of God. They may do so personally or delegate the responsibility to a conscientious member, so that everything may be done at the proper time* (RB, 47). Parents, like the abbot, set up the schedule for family members and call them to it. We can ask the help of a conscientious member in the family to keep us to our schedule. This helper might be an older child who reminds the younger ones what they should be doing. Tasks like this help big brother or sister learn leadership and responsibility.

The daily schedule helps bring order to the family: every day presents many times, including a time to wake up, time to pray, time to eat, time to study, time to work, time to read, time to relax, and finally, time to sleep. Such times offer families familiar guideposts to help support our lives as individuals as well as our lives within the family. The strength and structure of a well-defined schedule holds us together but if it is too rigid, it will crack under the strain of the variety and unpredictability of life.

A second monastic principle for managing family life is flexibility. No one yet has arrived at the perfect family schedule. We are all journeying toward greater maturity in our lives together. Describing how monks are to live while traveling away from the abbey, Benedict instructs, *So too, those who have been sent on a journey are not to omit the prescribed hours but to observe them as best they can, not neglecting their measure of service* (RB, 50). Applying this wisdom to family life today, parents are wise to stick to their family schedule as much as possible in whatever circumstance they might find themselves. At the same time, we know that situations arise that require flexibility. In such situations, we do "as best we can," and don't get upset about adjusting the family schedule a little.

When either extreme of rigidity or passivity becomes part of the schedule, the family suffers. Passivity allows others outside the family to dictate priorities for family members. Without a clear family schedule, a passive family will be pulled apart by many demands and desires. Other families err on the side of rigidity, allowing no room for flexibility within the family schedule. Some parents put up such protective walls around their children that they have little opportunity to grow or risk failure. Children who are raised with an overly rigid family schedule or with no family schedule at all learn self-doubt, insecurity, and irresponsibility. Children who are raised within a healthy, flexible family schedule grow in self-esteem, leadership, and love.

Today, we live amid disorder in many forms. Bad habits seem easier to form than good patterns of living. Multiple demands pull us in too many directions at once. In spite of our family calendar, with all its lists and schedules, our family life has often teetered out of balance, with too many conflicting demands pulling us away from our life together. Establishing and maintaining healthy patterns for the family takes constant effort and perseverance. We might need to give ourselves a push every now and then because we are resistant to change. Over time, we begin to see that change is truly possible. Through quality family time together, every family can experience renewal and transformation.

Drop Everything and Read

As our kids were growing up, we spent a half hour reading aloud to them at bedtime almost every night. This family habit has carried us over seas, beyond the stars, back in time, and through wonderful adventures of the human imagination. In nearly three decades of parenting we've read aloud hundreds of the greatest works of literature for children and youth. We've journeyed with the hobbit Bilbo to Smaug's lair, flown with Peter Pan to Never, Never Land, climbed the Alps with Heidi, entered the secret garden with Mary, and built shelters with Robinson Crusoe on his shipwrecked island.

Such regular reading time is known in many homes as "Drop Everything and Read" time (D.E.A.R.). When we drop everything and read, we like to mix our selections, including fiction and nonfiction, fantasy and biography, poetry and prose. Though occasional reading is better than no reading, best of all is a family habit of regular reading in the home. We develop this habit by giving the family set reading hours and encouraging all family members to read on their own. Even while backpacking as a family in Olympic National Park on family vacations, we read aloud at bedtime in our tents.

In the monastery, reading is a daily activity. Benedict recommended a focused, attentive atmosphere amongst the listeners. *Let there be complete silence. No whispering, no speaking — only the reader's voice should be heard there. . . . Monastics will read and sing, not according to rank, but according to their ability to benefit their hearers* (RB, 38). Though illiteracy was widespread in his day, Benedict insisted upon teaching all monks to read, regardless of their social rank when they entered the monastery. He called all monks to spend several hours a day silently reading, and scheduled several times every day for reading aloud to the whole community.

During daily reading time, children are encouraged to listen attentively to stories. Parents assist by removing distractions as well as by choosing books that are age appropriate and engaging to your child. During read-aloud time, we've sometimes refocused busy children by allowing them to draw pictures or quietly build Legos while listening to the story.

Family reading is family nourishment. Good books are food for the mind and soul. Besides reading classic children's literature to our children, we've also regularly read stories from a children's Bible aloud as a family. Like developing any new habit, making space and giving time each day for reading takes a lot of effort at first. Once the habit is formed in your family, everyone will look forward to this time. We found that reading right before bedtime works the best for our family. In the *Exercises* section at the back of this chapter, you'll find a list of resources for choosing good books to read aloud in your home, as well as a more detailed outline for enjoying D.E.A.R. time in your home.

Over the years, we've purchased books for our children as birthday and Christmas gifts. We want our children to leave our home as adults with their own mini-library of great books. We also ask others, including friends, grandparents, and teachers, what books they've enjoyed reading to their children and grandchildren. When families establish healthy reading habits early on, they will nourish the family through years and generations.

Quiet Time

The most surprising quality I've encountered on my annual retreats at the monastery has been the sense of quiet within the cloister. Maybe it is the contrast to the noisy reality of busy family life; maybe the withdrawal from traffic, music, and media; or perhaps it is leaving my word-oriented profession to enter the quiet of the abbey. Monastic quiet is almost tangible. The air itself seems full, expectant, listening. One night after Compline, I was bounding up the stairs two at a time, hurrying to my room in the retreat house at the monastery. A quiet inner voice spoke, almost audibly, saying, "Why the hurry? Slow down. Enter the quiet."

As I lay in my bed that night, I listened to frogs in the pond outside my window. They joined together into a monastic choir, swelling in voice and volume. Suddenly, they were quiet. Silence filled the air. Then one frog ventured forth in song. A few others joined in, until the whole company once again joined the anthem. This repeated rhythm of song and silence struck a deep chord in my spirit that night. I believe God created our lives for the regular rhythm of words and silence.

Benedict advised that *Monastics should diligently cultivate silence at all times, but especially at night* (RB, 42). Drawing upon the wisdom of the *Rule,* families do well to plant silence into the family schedule. Like the "quiet old lady whispering 'Hush'" in Brown's classic *Goodnight Moon,* there are times in every home when busy families need the gift of quiet. Without quiet time in the family, parents and children become weary, unfocused, and disjointed. Bringing in a brief daily time of quiet in a home can move the family toward a calm center. From the start, even while children are infants, plan for times of silence in the family. Families that learn to "enter the quiet" by encouraging quiet time in the home will deepen in their love for God and one another.

Bedtime Rituals

I appreciate the practicality of Benedict's bedtime instructions. In the *Rule,* he offers a list of mundane bedtime instructions: *sleep in separate beds; a lamp must be kept burning in the room until morning; sleep clothed; always be ready to arise without delay when the signal is given; the younger members should not have their beds next to each other; on arising, quietly encourage each other, for the sleepy like to make excuses* (RB, 22). It may seem strange to find such ordinary daily instructions in one of the great classics of Western literature. Benedictine spirituality blossoms in the ordinary places of life, such as bedtime.

One of the simple gifts we give our children is the gift of a regular bedtime. We set our children's bedtime according to the age of the child (toddlers versus teens), the day of the week (school nights versus non-school nights), and the time of the year (summer versus winter). Children will perform at a higher level in school and in life if they've had proper rest. In general, children require more sleep than adults. Besides offering our children healthy bodies and alert minds through training of regular sleep habits, we also create a secure environment for our children through regular bedtime rituals.

Though they usually resist bedtime, children love bedtime rituals. Our kids took their time getting ready for bed. I was amazed at how much fun they had simply brushing their teeth. I've walked in to find six clowns in that bathroom, our three sons and their mirror images, creating a silly circus for their own nightly entertainment. Even older children and teens desire bedtime rituals that offer comfort to their weary, anxious souls. After being pushed and pulled by the busy events of the day, we need the safety and comfort of bedtime rituals to help us get to sleep.

After establishing a regular bedtime we can use a few other tools to assist us in helping our children sleep in peace. These include a night light, comfortable bedding, and the removal of distractions. Benedict insisted upon keeping a night light in the monastic dormitories until morning. I believe children of any age should be allowed to have a night light for comfort. Even parents are afraid of the dark at times. Offering a little prayer and a little light can usually relieve fear of the dark. We are wise to provide our kids with a comfortable bed. The most important piece of furniture you will ever buy as a parent is a child's mattress. We spend at least one-third of our lives in bed. See that children do not keep each other awake well after lights-out with games and giggles. If necessary, separate children who are overly noisy or busy at night.

Some positive ways to focus children at bedtime include reading, music, and prayer. Besides reading aloud at bedtime, we've enjoyed singing our children to sleep with lullabies and songs of faith, hope and love. The last sound a child loves to hear before sleep is mom or dad's voice. Before they go to sleep, tell your children you love them, and ask God to protect them and keep them through the night. We've made it a regular nightly habit to put our hands upon our sleeping children's heads and ask God to watch over them. Thus, as parents we "lie down and sleep in peace, for in God alone our children dwell in safety."[47]

Work and Study

Work is a gift to our body and our soul. We are given the gift of work to improve our lives and the lives of others, to build up our lives, our family, our community, and our world. Like all of God's gifts, work can easily be misused. Too much work can be harmful to our body as well as our soul. All wise work is done in moderation, with the understanding that we were made for love. Work is one more tool God places in our hands to teach us to grow in love.

According to Benedict, *Idleness is the enemy of the soul. Therefore, the community members should have specified periods for manual labor as well as for prayerful reading* (RB, 48). Monks work with body and soul, including physical or manual labor as well as the mental or spiritual work of study. Two to three hours a day are devoted to reading and study in a Benedictine monastery. Both the practices of physical work and prayerful study are powerful antidotes to idleness. As a young student in Rome, Benedict became distressed by the busy distractions of the city and the idle pursuits of his fellow classmates. He fled into the hills and spent several years in solitude, learning to pray and meditate. The ancient Benedictine pattern of meditation is what we today would call study. Meditation includes memorization, mental reflection, and oral recitation of a passage of Scripture. With his commitment to the discipline of study, Benedict quietly revolutionized Western society. Every monk was required to learn to read and write. Manuscripts were copied and recopied, making available enough books for daily reading within the abbey. From these seedlings of study grew some of the great trees of Western civilization, including libraries, schools, universities, and increased literacy among the common population.

When people are idle, they easily lose a sense of purpose and direction in their lives. Without the daily family habits of work and study we entertain boredom, as though saying, "Come on in, make yourself at home." Inner emptiness can lead us to chase after short-term pleasures, try to fill our lives with busy activities, and grasp at the wind in hopes of getting some direction.

In our family we picked a certain hour of the day for study time. During this time, we expected our kids to keep on task. Children are easily distracted. If they were found wasting time, being lazy, or disturbing others, they faced warnings, removal to another room, and other forms of training. Even those who are sick or young can share in work and study. We show our children the importance of set periods for work and study by modeling this in our own lives. As we immerse ourselves in our daily work and study, we will find an inner sense of purpose flowing from our lives.

Within the home, work is part of the daily rhythm of family life. Children love learning to work. They will whine and complain at first. But once they see that their work matters to their parents and to the family, they begin to take pride in doing a good job. As parents we teach our children how to work, especially how to begin and finish set tasks. This is as true with teenagers as it is with two-year-olds. There are simple tasks that two-year-olds can accomplish, while discovering in the process that they too have something to offer the family.

During the two or three decades parents share with children at home, one of the great gifts we give our children is a healthy work ethic, including a love for study. It takes persistence, over months and years, to teach children the value of work and study. Whether we're in the middle of test week during the school year or away on a camping trip in the summer, study is one of the heartbeat activities of our daily family life. Study stretches the mind and spirit to better understand God, people, and the universe in which we live. Through study of nature, we discover more of the beauty and creative genius surrounding our lives, a mystery that even dwells deep within our own body and spirit.

In the *Exercises* at the end of this chapter, you'll find some specific ways to develop the healthy habit of study in your family. Whether in work or in study, we participate with God in re-creative activity, bringing goodness to our world. When we see our work and study in the light of divine handiwork, our lives will develop greater balance and beauty.

Creativity and Play

Benedictine monasteries are havens of creativity. I've met stained-glass artists, bookbinders, potters, gourmet cooks, writers, musicians, and Bonsai masters, all within the walls of Benedictine monasteries. Benedict says *If there are artisans in the monastery, they are to practice their craft with all humility* (RB, 57). Monks are encouraged to develop their creative gifts "with all humility." Family spirituality also encourages the creative gifts of children, recognizing that all creativity is a gift from God. In the family we are wise to support our children in the pursuit of their unique artistic talents or skills. Children are naturally artistic. We make provision for this natural aptitude for creativity within the family by providing tools and training, by making space in the home for artistic expression, and through encouraging our children to explore many ways to be creative. I believe every human is a creative person, made in the image of the Master Artist. For many people, their creativity lies dormant like "Sleeping Beauty," awaiting the prince to come and wake her with a kiss. Parents who encourage creativity in the home offer such a "waking kiss" to the creative spirit within their children.

Through the years, our home has become something like an art gallery. The walls are filled with color, design, and beauty. When our kids bring home artwork, we

encourage them to add their creativity to the growing collection in our home art gallery. Two of our sons
received their college degrees in fine art. Their paintings and nature photographs are on display throughout
our home. Our youngest son, Thomas, now in his early
twenties, has dedicated himself to capturing the beauty
of nature through the lens of his digital camera.[48] We've
been richly blessed with beauty.

Play and creativity are more than just frivolity; they
can create a foundation for the future course of a person's life. Often a childhood hobby will grow into a
life vocation. My older brother, Mike, created amazing paper airplanes and imaginative drawings when we
were children. Today he is head of a European design
company in Italy. When children are encouraged to create and explore their artistic life, as adults they will
carry that confidence into their professional careers.

One of the greatest forms of creativity in children is
their sense of play. Dr. Jeff Sigafoos, professor of Education at the University of Tasmania, makes the following
playful remark about the creativity of children: "Play
is the business of childhood and it would be fair to say
that most children love their job."[49] Though play may
not be the main business of a monastery, the monks I've
met have always expressed a deep sense of playfulness
and laughter. A common stereotype of monastic life is
one of serious, silent men shuffling through dark halls
on their way to the next worship service. In my experience, monks are full of joy and playfulness. It is true
that Benedict was against harmful forms of speech and

destructive jokes, but good humor and joy are a normal monastic way of life.

C. S. Lewis mentions four types of laughter in his book *The Screwtape Letters*. "I divide the causes of human laughter into Joy, Fun, the Joke Proper, and Flippancy." Joy, according to Lewis, is "the serious business of heaven." Fun is "closely related to joy," and "it promotes charity, courage, contentment."[50] Lewis warns us that the Joke Proper and Flippancy can easily divert us from heaven and dull our spiritual senses. We all have heard jokes that play upon people's prejudice, fears, and corrupt thoughts. These are not part of family spirituality. Joy and Fun on the other hand build up the family and nurture our childlike life with God.

When children grow up with creativity and play, they gain an inner confidence and freedom to create as adults, thus bringing beauty and goodness to their work and to the people around them.[51] At all ages, compassion, community building, love, and forgiveness are the highest forms of creative living. Through creativity and play, these highest forms of artistry awaken within us.

Time Together and Time Apart

More than ever before in human history, families are on the move. Parents travel by planes to distant cities for business and pleasure. Children travel by bus or car to distant towns for sports and music events. Extended families are spread out across continents. Often, families find their life together pulled apart by a variety of events and commitments.

Before I leave on an overnight trip I hug my kids, tell them I love them and will pray for them, and ask them to pray for me. This simple act of faith unites our hearts even though miles separate us. Spiritual life in the home is a gift from God to knit the family together, regardless of schedule and place. Many families today face times of separation due to careers, military service, or other circumstances. When our family is divided by distance, we still share life together and unite our hearts across miles. Benedict offers this wise guidance to families while apart: *Those who have been sent on a journey are not to omit the prescribed hours but to observe them as best they can, not neglecting their measure of service* (RB, 50). Habits of the heart unite a family in the bond of faith, hope, and love. When we set aside time to pray for one another, God weaves our hearts together when apart.

Two common parenting problems arise when discussing time apart: overprotection and abandonment. Overprotective parents, also known as "helicopter" parents, hover over their children, never wanting to leave them out of fear of what may happen when they are out of sight. Children of overprotective parents grow up with insecurity and enter adulthood lacking confidence to face the challenges of the world outside. Parents are sometimes called to travel away from their families to attend to work or extended family commitments in another place. Though family life may be disrupted for a time, healthy families can handle this separation and even grow stronger through such trials. Family spirituality unites a family while apart, helping to preserve the integrity of the family though apart for a time.

The problem more common in our day is abandonment. Busy parents who spend too much time away from
the family will have difficulty maintaining a healthy
home life. When a career demands a father or mother
to abandon their parenting to the care of professionals,
I believe that career needs to be seriously reconsidered.
In the past fifty years, with the increase of opportunities for working women in society, many mothers
have entered the marketplace. In the balancing act
of dual-career homes, both fathers and mothers must
learn to make career sacrifices for the sake of their
children. While professional child-care workers may
provide excellent care for our children, the life work
of raising children belongs primarily to parents, not to
professionals.

Neither overprotection nor abandonment help children grow up in love. Better to invest our children with
the gift of love, faith, and trust, whether we are together
or apart. Time together also asks for time apart. Healthy
parents allow creative space in the home for solitude as
well as intentional times for shared family life. We do
not need to smother our kids. Neither do we need to
abandon them.

Benedict instructs that *Members sent on a journey will
ask the abbot and community to pray for them* (RB, 67).
Every time we go out on a long family trip, we sing a
travel prayer. We learned the melody from my Finnish
sister-in-love, and wrote the words early in our marriage. We sing this travel song at the beginning of every
long trip we take.

Travel Song

Guide us safely on our way,
Hold us in your hand we pray,
May your presence with us be.
Father, go with us today.

Lord, we've only just begun,
Keep us from the evil one,
May your presence with us be.
Go with us beloved Son.

Holy Spirit, fill our hearts,
To our ears your Word impart,
May your presence with us be.
Go with us now as we start.

In our family, when someone goes away on a trip, we pray for each other. While separated by travels, we remember one another in prayer, asking God to watch over us. God is not bound to a certain place. God goes with us whether we are aware of this or not. As the ancient songwriter declares, "If I rise on the wings of the dawn, if I settle on the far side of the sea, ever there your hand will guide me, your right hand will hold me fast."[52] When we return, we give thanks to God for bringing us back together. Anyone in the family who leaves home without giving notice lets the whole family down. I believe that children need to ask parents for permission to travel. As parents, we are wise to give notice to one another and to children for all our travels.

When we need to spend time apart from our family, we've recited an ancient Jewish blessing: "May the

Lord keep watch between you and me, when we are away from each other."[53] We say a short prayer and say farewell with hugs and kisses. When we return home, we embrace one another and give thanks to God for bringing the family together once more. Children need parents who keep calling the family together daily, weekly, and monthly, to enjoy quality time together as a family. Parents need to encourage their children to take risks by sending them out with others into creative ventures. Whether the family is together or away, as parents we nurture *life-together* habits that unite our lives across miles and years with faith, hope, and love.

FAMILY LIFE TOGETHER EXERCISES

EXERCISE 1: Children's Booklists

Over the years, parents and grandparents have asked me for guidance in selecting age-appropriate books for children. Below I've listed book resources to assist you in selecting books to read aloud to your children. Choose one or two of these to add to your parenting resource shelf.

- Betsy Hearne, *Choosing Books for Children* (University of Illinois Press, 2000, 3rd Revision).

- Gladys Hunt, *Honey for a Child's Heart* (Grand Rapids: Zondervan, 1969).

- William Kilpatrick, *Books that Build Character: A Guide to Teaching Your Child Moral Values Through Stories* (New York: Touchstone, 1994).

- Madeleine L'Engle, *Trailing Clouds of Glory* (Philadelphia: Westminster, 1985).

- Mary Leonhardt, *99 Ways to Get Kids to Love Reading: and 100 Books They'll Love* (Crown Publishers, 1997).

- Valerie V. Lewis and Walter M. Mayes, *Valerie & Walter's Best Books for Children: A Lively, Opinionated Guide* (New York: Avon, 1998).

- Twila Liggett, *Reading Rainbow Guide to Children's Books* (New York: Carol Publishing Group, 1994).

- Eden Ross Lipson, *The New York Times Parent's Guide to the Best Books for Children* (Three Rivers Press, 2000, 3rd Revision).

EXERCISE 2: D.E.A.R. Time

This exercise offers families step by step guidance for enjoying D.E.A.R. time in your family life together: D.E.A.R. time simply means time to "Drop Everything and Read."

What to read

- Choose books that are age appropriate. If you have children in a wide range of ages, you may consider having separate reading times for younger and older children.

- Collect book suggestions from family members and friends to be read-aloud at D.E.A.R. time. Check children's booklists for good ideas (see above).

- Begin your D.E.A.R. time with a fun book that catches everyone's attention.

- Over the years, broaden your children's reading diet, including picture books, fairy tales, folk tales, historical fiction, contemporary fiction, fantasy and science fiction, and biography. Keep expanding your children's vocabulary, imagination, and horizons through time together in good books. We have read aloud hundreds of books to our three sons, beginning with such books as *Goodnight Moon* (32 pages; total of 130 words), by Margaret Wise Brown when they were in preschool; and *Les Miserables* (1200 pages) by Victor Hugo, when they were in high school.

- Read aloud stories from a children's Bible, our soul's finest feast!

When to read

- At a family meeting ask the family to agree upon a set amount of reading time each week. For example, "Our family promises to read aloud every Tuesday and Thursday evening for 30 minutes, just before bedtime."

- We found the half hour just before lights out worked well in our family life over the years.

- If you've never had a read-aloud time in your home before, begin with a small amount of time, even five or ten minutes. Read a picture book or a chapter of a chapter book, depending on the age of your children.

How to read

◆ At first, a parent should be the D.E.A.R. time reader. After this habit is set, share reading duties with various members of the family. Benedict encouraged the choice of a reader who had the *ability to benefit their hearers.*

◆ Do not allow children to disrupt the reader. Some children who are very active may need additional assistance in listening to the story. We've allowed our children to quietly draw, doodle, or build with Legos while listening.

◆ Better to finish the D.E.A.R. time with your children wanting more than to bore them to distraction. Read-aloud time should be enjoyable and kept short enough to make children want to hear more.

EXERCISE 3: Flower Beds of Quiet

Like planting flowers in a flowerbed, give your children the beauty of set times for quiet. Within these "flower boxes" of quiet, fragrant flowers will bloom. If anyone in our home insists upon talking during times of quiet, especially nighttime quiet, we gently remind them that it is quiet time. Families that respect silence learn to weigh words and speak the truth to one another in love. Families that have a habit of quiet times offer a fragrance of love to others through their speech. Here are some ideas for planting flowerbeds of quiet times in the family:

◆ quiet play times in the morning for preschoolers;

◆ quiet resting and reading time in the afternoon;

- quiet study time in the evening for school-age children;

- quiet listening time during night stories;

- quiet time alone with God daily in Scripture and prayer;

- quiet observation time on a long trip together;

- quiet thinking and praying time at lights out.

EXERCISE 4: Bedtime Rituals

Children love regular bedtime rituals. If you currently do not have a regular pattern at bedtime for your child, try implementing such practices for a week or two. At first, your child will resist, wanting the flexibility to do as he or she pleases. After a few days, you will find your child settling into the new pattern and finding delight in bedtime rituals. The regular habits at bedtime in our home have included the following:

- Take care of personal hygiene: brushing teeth; getting a drink of water; using the toilet.

- Change into bedclothes, including putting away day clothes.

- Say goodnight to family with kisses and hugs.

- Read stories together.

- Enjoy short night devotions: read a paragraph from a children's Bible and pray together.

- Say a nighttime blessing. We say Psalm 4:8 together: "I will lie down and sleep in peace, for you alone, O LORD, make me dwell in safety."

Other nighttime benedictions include:

* The LORD bless you and keep you; the LORD make his face shine upon you.[54]

* May God keep you from all harm and watch over your life.[55]

* Dwell in the shelter of the Most High; rest in the shadow of the Almighty.[56]

* The last bedtime ritual is what we call quiet time: lights go out; hands and bodies come to rest; heads are on pillows; we quiet our thoughts and offer our silent prayers.

EXERCISE 5: Five Ways of Study

Among the many forms of study, enjoy meditation, reading, Bible study, journaling, and nature study. Try implementing one or more of these forms of study in your life as a family.

1. *Meditation*. In meditation we turn away from distractions and fix our full attention upon God. The Psalmist encourages us to meditate upon Scripture and nature. Meditation is drinking from God's well of living water, as written in the book of Isaiah: "With joy you will draw water from the wells of salvation."[57] This well is available daily as we enter the silence of God through meditation.

2. *Reading*. Reading is another form of study. Children love regular trips to the library. Let them obtain books that interest them. Place books in their

lives that will stretch them and help them grow up in love. If possible, make time each day for reading. Many other demands will try to steal away reading time. Read great stories to your children. Give them books for their birthdays so that they too may begin to build their library.

3. *Bible Study.* I believe the Bible is our first and best source for family study. Here are some ideas we've found helpful for reading the Bible: Read the Bible daily. Read the Bible slowly. Read a book of the Bible from start to finish. Try a daily Bible reading plan. Reap a harvest of wisdom from studying the Bible using the following outline for study:

   R: Read — read a passage of the Bible;

   E: Explore — explore what the author is saying, including the themes, people, events and principles;

   A: Apply — apply certain principles and truths from the passage to your life;

   P: Pray/Practice — put into practice what you learned, asking God to change your life through study.

4. *Journaling.* We're wise to keep a journal and encourage our children to do the same. We easily forget from one season to the next the important lessons we've learned. Through a journal, we can more quickly review what we've studied and learned. I keep a written record of dreams, poems, thoughts, lists of fears and hopes,

conflicts and resolutions, and prayers. We have regularly given journals to our children, and we encourage them to write, draw, and record their life experiences.

5. *Study nature.* The study of nature can be an experience of delight and adventure. Unfortunately today, too many children are foreigners to the whole world of nature. Electronic entertainment and personal computers in the home have replaced outdoor play of yesteryear. Richard Louv, journalist and author of *Last Child in the Woods: Saving our Children from Nature-Deficit Disorder,* articulates the dangers of raising children who are disconnected from the outdoors. According to Louv, one of the healthiest choices parents can make with their children is regular time spent exploring the outdoors and enjoying the gift of nature.[58] Here are a few ideas for family study of nature:

    ◆ Take nature walks together, collecting creatures in a bug box or leaves and flowers in a press.

    ◆ Grow a garden or a pot of edible herbs.

    ◆ Do simple home science experiments.[59]

    ◆ Invest in tools for nature study: a digital camera, binoculars, waterproof hiking boots, camping gear, nature books and topographical maps are some tools for nature study we've included in recent years.

- No purchases are necessary for the observation and study of nature. All we really need is a pair of eyes and an inquiring mind. Within the family, such study becomes a doorway into the world of nature, filling our children's spirit with wonder and adventure.

EXERCISE 6: Family Art School

Help children explore a whole variety of creative arts. In your family try exploring together one of the forms of art below. Sign up for art classes together in your community. Buy a beginning book on one of these forms of creativity. Or ask an older person to teach you and your child one of these creative skills.

Creative arts for families

- writing, speaking, storytelling, dramatizing;
- cooking, homemaking, gardening, designing;
- making melody, harmony, rhythm, and composing;
- weaving, knitting, embroidering, sewing;
- healing, mending, repairing, restoring;
- acting, directing, dancing, choreographing;
- inventing, programming, translating, structuring;
- role-playing, game-playing, laughter-making, delight-taking.

EXERCISE 7: Family Play and Laughter

In our family life together, play and laughter are a part of our daily diet, just as important as milk and bread.

When we run out of milk, we run to the market. What do we do when we run out of laughter? Below is a list of ten ideas that might help restore play and laughter in your family:

1. Set aside daily time in the home for play. We've even dedicated several rooms in our home to games and play. Our kids have always loved playing with Legos. We have an old bunk bed in our son's bedroom that has become a Lego twin-city, populated by hundreds of little Lego people.

2. Get on the same level as your children to play with them, a few minutes every day.

3. Enjoy one night a week as "Family Game Night." For the first few years, when our children were all in preschool or elementary school, everyone in the family chose a different game. We still love to play family games together including card games and board games. On a recent visit to our married son and daughter-in-love, we enjoyed a family game night that included a board game, a family computer game, hide-and-seek, and a lane of bowling at the local bowling alley.

4. Read funny stories aloud together. Reread those books and stories that tickled your family funny bone in the past.

5. Use media for family play. Watch the classic comedians, like the Three Stooges or Charlie Chaplin. Enjoy Pixar animated movies. Listen to

humorists such as Garrison Keillor while driving in the car together.

6. Develop inside family jokes that build family members up and draw upon family memories. The running joke is common in many families, a type of humor that brings up laughter in the family at odd moments.

7. Find playful ways to communicate serious lessons and family training.

8. Celebrate special days with games and fun. We've enjoyed sending our children on a treasure hunt on their birthdays to find their presents. There were always as many clues as years.

9. Get outside into God's good creation and take delight together in the simple wonders of nature.

10. Touch and tickle, play "gotch'ya last," wrestle on the carpet, hug each other, and kiss one another goodnight. Our bodies are designed by God to offer us many ways to express love and delight.

Chapter Six

Become the Welcome

Embracing the Basics
of Hospitality

Let mutual love continue. Do not neglect to show hospitality to strangers, for by doing that some have entertained angels without knowing it.
— Hebrews 13:1–2 (NRSV)

When I've visited a European cathedral I've often had the feeling that the inside is bigger than the outside. Step through the door of any cathedral and look up into the high vaulted ceilings and the brilliance of the rose windows. Family spirituality, like a cathedral, invites us to step into a life of hospitality. We can practice hospitality in a way that welcomes strangers and friends into our hearts — hearts that are expansive, open places filled with love and light. The more space we make for God in our hearts, the greater capacity we have to welcome others into our lives. In chapter six we will explore ways of Benedictine hospitality. As you bring these practices into your family life you will discover greater capacity for welcoming others.

Welcoming Guests

Living in a time of tremendous unrest and instability in early sixth-century Italy, Benedict had the boldness to warmly welcome strangers at his monastery gates. *All guests who present themselves are to be welcomed as Christ* (RB, 53). The monasteries that sprouted up across the landscape of Europe became places of true refuge and welcome for the busy, the weary, the poor, and the homeless. Anyone who needed a bed and a meal was welcomed, not merely as another mouth to feed, but as though God himself had asked for a night's lodging.

Hospitable homes offer love to guests in practical ways, regardless of their wealth or status, without showing favoritism. Throughout the Bible, we read about God's heart of mercy for the poor, the widow, the outcast, and anyone in need. Benedict echoes this concern. *Great care and concern are to be shown in receiving poor people and pilgrims, because in them more particularly Christ is received; our very awe of the rich guarantees them special respect* (RB, 53). Benedictine monasteries today always feature a guesthouse to welcome guests, putting into practice the principles of hospitality taught by Benedict in the *Rule* fifteen centuries ago. Every time I've visited a monastery, I've been warmly welcomed by the monks and made to feel as though my life was greatly valued.

Family spirituality invites us to give special place in our hearts not only to friends and relatives, but also to the poor, the homeless, and the needy. Many families seldom welcome any guests into their homes and teach their children to be afraid of all unknown people. While we are wise to teach our children caution in relating to strangers, when we close our hearts to every unfamiliar face, we may end up shutting out extraordinary gifts sent by God. It may be that we have become too protective of our privacy and are closing the door to God's surprising love.

I'm not claiming that hospitality is easy work. On the contrary, welcoming guests is usually an interruption to the family schedule. We've been roused at 3:00 a.m. by a single mom with little children, fleeing from an abusive boyfriend. We've been unexpectedly called upon to house foreigners who have stayed in our home for days or weeks until they could settle into more permanent housing. Twenty years ago we opened our door to a foreign student at the university where I worked at the time. That friendship led to many other wonderful relationships with internationals. We now have family all over the globe. We've welcomed students, teachers, actors and artists into our home for meals and overnight stays including people from Germany, France, Switzerland, Japan, Sudan, China, and Morocco. Whether for a night or a season, hospitality can be hard work, throwing off our established family rhythms and impinging on our freedom.

No wonder St. Peter encourages us to "offer hospitality to one another without grumbling."[60] After guests leave, there is often something to grumble about, including dirty dishes, soiled linens, and neglected household chores. Sometimes, it's easier to refuse hospitality than open the door and welcome a guest. One of our challenges as parents has been to preserve family unity, while welcoming others into the family circle. As much as possible, we like to include guests in the life of the family. This might mean asking guests to help prepare meals, share in chores, and join with us in our family spirituality. When we share our life and faith with relatives, friends and guests, we allow people to journey with us, bringing to us their gifts of laughter, encouragement and love. We affirm the presence of God in their lives as we practically share the love of God through the gift of our open heart and home.

Nurture of Parents

Twin dangers face families in the work of hospitality: first, to neglect to care for others simply because it is too demanding; second, to forget to care for ourselves because we are too busy. Just as children and guests need care, so do parents. Hospitality, like parenting, can be tiring work. Benedict makes special provision for the leader of the monastery, the abbot, especially during mealtimes. Parents, like abbots, need to care for themselves in order to best care for their family. In the course of welcoming and serving others, there comes a time when we begin to get weary. As important as it is to have everyone together for meals, there are times when parents need an evening away to enjoy time together without children.

We've regularly entrusted our children to a competent sitter and taken time to nurture our relationship. Over the past few years, I've asked a wise mentor to check in on me every week, to see if I've taken my wife out on a date. My wife and I both work outside the home. Many years ago, we arranged our schedule during the school year in order to have Fridays together for rest and renewal. This allows for one day a week in which we can nurture our love life apart from our children. I know of a married couple who arrange child care for their children in order to take day hikes together without kids. Our marriages require care. Parents are wise to spend at least one meal away from their children every month. During this meal out, share with one another the joys and burdens of your hearts, your dreams and your passions, while you take delight in a mini-vacation from the stresses of parenting.

Single parents also need time away from child-rearing to get out with other friends for support and encouragement. Share child care with other adults. Develop a circle of friends with whom you will journey through life. Nurture your spirit. Instruct your mind. Feed your soul. Exercise your body. Then you will have refreshment and energy to be present fully to your children and to reach out with compassion to others in your life. To refuse to offer the gift of welcome to others shuts off the flow of love into the family. To neglect caring for our lives through daily, weekly, and monthly time away from our children opens the door to depression, burnout, and resentment. So take a little time every day, an evening a month, and a weekend a year to nurture yourself outside of your life with your children.

Long-Term Guests and Adoption

I served for six years as a campus pastor at a state university in Tennessee. During that time, we welcomed a variety of long-term guests into our home as live-in residents. No matter who they were, they brought extra challenges and delights into our home life. Opening our home to strangers, including long-term guests, is a natural extension of love in family life together. Hospitality to strangers is part of the warp and woof of society in many parts of the world. Americans have a lot to learn from our Mexican, Middle Eastern, and African neighbors about the practice of hospitality.

Benedict offers the following insights concerning the reception of long-term guests. *Provided that they are content with the life as they find it, and do not make excessive demands that upset the monastery, but are simply content with what they find, they should be received for as long a time as they wish* (RB, 61). Many families receive such long-term guests as an elderly relative, a grandchild, an in-law, a foreign exchange student, a needy neighbor, a step-family member, a foster child, or a college student. We have several honorary "family members" who have come to live with us for a week, a month or longer. While seeking to involve longer-term guests in the life of our family, we benefit from the unique gifts that they share with our family. As Benedict observes, *It is possible that God guided them [to you] for this very purpose* (RB, 61).

Adoption is another form of long-term hospitality. Too many children in our world have no home and no family. Adoption is one creative response to this problem. When we choose to adopt a child, we offer a home and loving family to this child as a personal, lifelong expression of love. Birth parents and adoptive parents work out the child's care through the mediation of an adoption agency. This care may include visitation and gift-giving privileges, legal guardianship, and spiritual care for the child. All these issues are worked out by wise counselors with the child's best interests in mind.

The care of orphaned children ranks high on God's list of spiritual habits. "Religion that God accepts as pure and faultless is this: to look after orphans and widows in their distress."[61] Such care of orphans can involve welcoming them into our home as our own children or helping to support orphanages in some other part of our needy world. When we look after unwanted children as though they are our own, no one promises they will love us in return. Adopted children can easily feel torn between their adoptive and birth parents. Adoption can be challenging but also an extremely rewarding expression of hospitality.

In Tolstoy's well-loved story "What Men Live By," the shoemaker and his wife welcome a stranger into their home only to discover years later that their guest was an angel sent to earth to learn certain lessons, including the truth that "all people live not by care for themselves but by love." At the end of the story, the angel recites the lessons he has learned from his time with the shoemaker and his wife. "I know now that people only seem to live when they care only for themselves, and that it is by

love for others that they really live. He who has Love
has God in him, and is in God — because God is Love."[62]

As a practical expression of our love, we welcome
long-term guests, including orphans and adopted children, loving them as we would like to be loved,
knowing we live "not by care for ourselves but by love."
Who knows when we will have the privilege of serving
homemade apple pie to one of God's undercover angels!

Friends and Mentors

One of the important things we do when we move into
a new community is to find a new circle of friends,
including a new family of faith. Our family has always
been surrounded by wise friends and mentors who have
helped us raise our children. These friends and mentors have included coaches, teachers, church members,
neighbors, and employers.

Every year, in the local church where I serve as pastor, parents bring their newborn children either to be
dedicated as children of God or to receive the sacra-
ment of baptism. When they stand before the people,
parents make public promises regarding their parenting,
including the daily care and guidance of their children.
The community of faith also makes a public promise
to support the family with love, prayers, and practical support. These promises are brought to life in the
weekly care we offer one another through friendship
and mentoring. There are many creative ways to mentor
or befriend families. All the ideas below are taken from
the pages of faithful people I know in our village:

+ Babysit little children while moms spend time together in study and prayer.

+ Invest time coaching youth sports.

+ Provide volunteer house-cleaning services for busy moms.

+ Gather children together after school for a weekly club to learn more about God.

+ Volunteer for the SMART reading program through the public elementary school.

+ Become a surrogate grandparent to children who live far away from their grandparents.

+ Give a week of vacation time to volunteer as a summer camp youth counselor.

+ Organize an annual community auction to raise support for a local childcare center.

+ Serve as a volunteer at the local pregnancy resource center to assist pregnant teens.

+ Help pack food backpacks to be given to hungry elementary school children every Friday for the weekend, so they will return on Monday alert and well fed.

Over the past three decades of my life as a pastor, I've been amazed and delighted to see the quality and variety of informal friendships and mentorships amongst parents and children in our local community. If you do not currently have a family of faith or friendships with other adults who are helping you raise your kids, you can begin today. Consider wise, trustworthy people in your life who already know your children. Consider also becoming a mentor to children in your community.[63] The gift of mentorship and friendship often comes through close friends who have had years of practice putting the love of God into action. Look for opportunities to welcome such friends and mentors into your family; they will deepen your family together.

The Heart of Parenting

When our family visited the Louvre in Paris and the Uffizi Gallery in Florence, we enjoyed viewing paintings of family life including such masterpieces as Michelangelo's "Holy Family" and Leonardo's "Virgin of the Rocks." Through twenty centuries, countless artists and sculptors have portrayed the heart of parenting through their depiction of Mary with Jesus. Mary reveals to us the heart of parenting, a spirituality of treasuring. At the birth of her son, we are told that "Mary treasured up all these things and pondered them in her heart."[64] Mary holds nearest to her heart the priceless gift of her unique child. I offer here a small gallery of ten portraits of this remarkable mother, each one revealing the heart of parenting, that of treasuring our children.

* We first see her as a young woman, probably a teenager, receiving the announcement from the angel Gabriel that she will give birth to the Son of the Most High.

- Next, we notice she is pregnant as she arrives at Elizabeth's home and celebrates in song God's great gift of life and blessing.

- We love the rustic portrait of Mary and Joseph in a stable with simple shepherd folks, delighting in the birth of their firstborn.

- Then, we observe her packing quickly in the night, fleeing as a fugitive, faithfully responding to the angel's warning in Joseph's dream.

- Years later, we share her panic-stricken heart when she loses her adolescent child in the big city and finally is reunited in the temple courtyard.

- We overhear her speaking to her grown son about the need for more wine at a wedding celebration and wonder as an abundance of excellent wine miraculously appears.

- We empathize with her as she tries to make sense of her son's fame and new career in light of all that God has promised.

- We grieve with her as she stands among other men and women, witnessing her son's crucifixion, death and burial.

- We rejoice with overwhelming joy at seeing her son alive again, uncertain if we can believe our eyes.

- Finally, we gather with her and the international family of faith to pray and wait for the coming gift of God's Spirit.[65]

On a week-long visit to a Benedictine monastery in Georgia twenty years ago, I walked from room to room, all around the abbey, meditating on pictures and sculptures of mother and child. My favorite piece soars high above the chancel, the vibrant-red rose window of Mary with child. In the upper corner of this window a dove descends and a hand reaches out of heaven. Filling the middle of the window we see Mary pregnant, meditating upon the mystery of God's treasure growing within her. As the morning sun rises, Mary radiates the beauty within her, as light fills the sanctuary.

Meditate upon your calling as a parent. A spirituality of treasuring enables our hearts to enjoy God's presence as we find delight in our children. The goal of parenting is to encourage each family member to grow in faith, hope and love. A spirituality of treasuring invites us to see all life, including the life of our child, as a gift from God. Along with Mary, we declare, "my soul gives glory to the Lord, my spirit delights in God."[66]

If Children Live with Praise

Benedict understood our lives as musical instruments. One of the great ancient songs played upon the instrument of the human soul for thousands of years is a single word, "Alleluia!"[67] Alleluia is an ancient Hebrew word for a shout of praise. Benedict instructed the monastic family to sing and declare this ancient word through the day and night, since it lifts the human spirit. When we sing or shout this word, we join our voice with generations of others who lifted up their hearts in praise before us. Every season offers us opportunity to join other fellow pilgrims in welcoming the art of praise in our home.

Why is praise such an important part of the human life? Like a standing ovation after a beautiful concert, our praise completes the symphony, echoing back to heaven what God has done for us here on earth. Praise brings the work of God full circle, allowing us to participate in the creative expression of joy. God created a good and beautiful world. We live to celebrate God in our lives.

When we teach our children to offer their praise, this simple act of faith overflows into our daily life as a family. As we lift our praise to God, grumpy hearts are gladdened, hard hearts are softened, angry hearts are quieted, and empty hearts are filled. Then we are able to offer words of encouragement and praise to others. There is an intimate connection between our words of praise to God and our words of praise to one another.

Children are reflections of the adults around them. If parents offer children criticism and shame, children will live a life of unkindness. If parents welcome the art of praise in the home, children will live a life of delight and learn to build others up. Dorothy Law Nolte, author of the well-loved poem "Children Learn What They Live," writes of parental praise:

Your words of praise encourage your children and make them feel deeply appreciated and valued. Praise nurtures their developing sense of self and helps them learn how to appreciate who they are, as well as who they're becoming. When we praise our children, we also provide them with a model for how to notice and express their appreciation of others and the world around them.[68]

As Nolte writes in her well-known poem, "If children live with praise, they learn appreciation."[69] We are wise to fill our homes with praise. Praise your children and help them learn to express praise when they arise and when they lie down, in their prayers and in their songs, through creative arts and through loving relationships. Deepening their own sense of appreciation will lead them to more fully appreciate and praise the goodness in others.

Service in the Community

I love the scene from *Little Women* in which the March sisters reluctantly share their Christmas breakfast with a poor family in the village. Before the needy family came into their lives, the March sisters were eagerly contemplating their plates of Christmas sweet breads and muffins. After giving away their feast to a truly needy family, they dance and laugh all the way home, full of the happiness that comes from serving others in love. There is great joy to be found in giving ourselves away to help others in need. Hospitality in the family flows in two directions: outward into the lives of needy people in our world; and inward into the heart of the family, filling us with God's goodness.

Some erroneously think that since monks have removed themselves from society they are uninvolved in acts of service. In my experience, monks live simple, prayerful, and industrious lives so that they will have an abundance to share with others in need. One of the ways monks serve others is through their hospitable welcome to guests who come for times of retreat. During these retreats, I've met many different monks who are appointed to serve guests by cooking, cleaning, gardening, teaching, praying, and by offering welcome and mentorship to strangers. The monastery is not a place of selfish isolation, but rather a center of service.

In a similar manner, the family is not a place for selfishness, grumbling, or fighting. The family is a place for loving service. When parents yield to selfish desires, they close the window blinds, shut out the light of love, and live in the dark. Nurturing a spirit of service within the family is difficult work that unfolds over time through persistent effort and a willingness to open the blinds and let in the light of love. As parents, we must be vigilant to nurture a spirit of service and love, especially through our own example.

How can a spirit of service be nurtured in children? Parents are wise to provide their children with a wide variety of hands-on service opportunities in the home, through the local community, and out in the world beyond their horizon. We've spent time as a family building homes for low-income families through Habitat for Humanity. We've collected gently worn clothes and shoes to take to Mexico where we've served the poor communities along the border. We've organized garage sales and other service projects to raise support for relief efforts after natural disasters have left thousands without hope. We've opened the church building as a community emergency shelter during a winter week-long power outage. Recently, a couple dozen concerned citizens and both churches in our village came together to form a food pantry to help feed the hungry in our area.

Families are wise to take children out into the community and into the wider world to experience firsthand the joy of serving others. As noted anthropologist Margaret Mead stated, "Never doubt that a small group of thoughtful, committed citizens can change the world; indeed, it's the only thing that ever has." A family that learns to serve others in love certainly has the potential to "change the world." When we go out as a family with full baskets to serve a needy world with love, we will come home with empty baskets and overflowing hearts.

FAMILY HOSPITALITY EXERCISES

EXERCISE 1: Welcoming Guests

As you enter the retreat wing at Gethsemani Abbey in Kentucky, you will see a bas-relief sculpture of a face and outstretched hands welcoming you with the words, *All guests are to be welcomed as Christ, for he will say, 'I was a stranger and you welcomed me'* (RB, 53). When we welcome guests into our home, according to Benedict, we are welcoming the presence of God into our lives. Thus, we seek to honor guests with loving service and an open heart. In the Benedictine practice of hospitality, guests are greeted with charity and open welcome, not suspicion or indifference. We put love into action through the gift of hospitality. This month, invite guests into your home and welcome them as though God is in your midst by putting into practice the following guidelines:

Guidelines for home hospitality

* Welcome guests at the door as you would welcome a highly honored person.

* Offer something to drink and a place at the family table.

* If they are overnight guests, provide a bed to sleep in and clean towels and linens.

* Invite your guests to join with you at mealtime as you give thanks to God.

* Share in good conversation, willing to open your hearts to them in love.

* Give your guests the gift of respect, privacy, and loving acceptance.

EXERCISE 2: Develop Your Family Hospitality Team

Train each member of the family in certain hospitality tasks, with time for practicing the skills of hospitality. Invite good friends over for a practice night, where everyone can try out their skills as members of the hospitality team. After the evening is over, offer praise and encouragement to each child for their part in offering hospitality to our friends. Here are some possible positions on the Hospitality Team:

* Greeter: welcomes people at the door, asks to take coats and hats;

* Host/Hostess: offers guests something to drink — or eat, depending on the occasion;

* Table Setter: helps set the table for a meal and lights the candles;

* Music & Fun: selects music for arrival and for meals;

* Entertainment: prepares fun activities for family and friends;

* Childcare provider: takes care of little ones, providing age-appropriate activities;

* Linens and Towels: puts out sets of clean towels and puts clean linens on beds;

* Kitchen Patrol: volunteers to help clear away dishes and clean up kitchen after meal;

* Chaplain: offers to pray at mealtimes and lead devotional times if appropriate.

EXERCISE 3: The Garden of Gratitude

Among the many forces that wrestle for the soul of the family, greed and gratitude are ever-present competitors for our attention. Greed demands more and more, never satisfied with what is given. Gratitude takes quiet delight in God's good gifts. Greed shouts; gratitude listens. Greed forces its way; gratitude willingly walks with another along their way. Greed cripples and imprisons; gratitude brings healing, beauty and newness of life. Spiritual parents seek to limit greed while nurturing gratitude. Opportunities arise weekly to place limits on greed. Enter a life of gratitude as a family with some of these steps.

Steps into the Garden of Gratitude

- Make homemade gifts rather than purchasing store-bought gifts.
- Mute TV commercials or simply turn the TV off.
- Refuse to buy into modern consumer appetites.
- Set actual dollar limits on luxury spending.
- Go without certain "necessary" items, especially when you think you can't.
- Choose one valuable possession each year and give it away to someone who will enjoy such a gift.
- Fast and pray, asking God to pull the roots of greed from the soul of your family.
- Explore creative ways to nurture gratitude.
- Share gifts you've received with others around you.
- Write thank-you notes.
- Go on family walks together.
- Grow a garden in the backyard and then give away vegetables to friends.
- Thank God for simple and natural gifts such as sun, laughter, and health.
- Daily, embrace someone in your family.

* Serve at your local rescue mission, food pantry or soup kitchen.
* Celebrate a special day with a feast and celebrate God's goodness.

EXERCISE 4: Parent Care

Family time together is vital for healthy families. Sometimes, though, parents should get away from their children. On a regular basis, healthy parents enjoy time together away from kids. Discover creative ways to nurture your relationship apart from kids. Circle your favorite three and plan time with one another this month.

* Light candles.
* Read poetry together.
* Go for walks to enjoy God's creation.
* Share your feelings with one another.
* Tickle and laugh together.
* Watch birds.
* Bake bread.
* Collect and press flowers.
* Go to garage sales or antique shops together.
* Every anniversary, recite your vows together.
* Write love letters to each other.
* Hold hands.
* Plan a date night at a favorite restaurant.
* Make love.
* Pray together.

EXERCISE 5: Opening the Family Treasure Chest

"By wisdom a house is built, and through understanding it is established; through knowledge its rooms are filled with rare and beautiful treasures."[70] The rarest and most beautiful treasures in our homes are our children. At the birth of Jesus, the Gospel of Luke tells us that Mary "treasured up all these things, pondering them in her heart."[71] Here are several ways to open the family treasure chest.

1. Learn the art of asking "open-ended" questions. Open-ended questions are those that do not have a right or wrong answer, but simply open the door for sharing of our lives. Such questions make your children the expert and you the learner.

2. Actively listen to your children's stories. Be slow to interject your opinions and viewpoints. Listen with your whole self, with your mind, heart and body. If your child is a toddler, sit on the floor to listen "eye to eye."

3. Spend regular quality time together. Go to the place where your children like to spend time. Sit with them on their beds. Watch their sports events. Have them teach you how to play their video games. Discover projects, activities, and common interests, which you can share together with your kids, especially child-oriented activities, as well as those that inspire imagination, creativity, and love.

4. Share life stories, values, morals and faith with your children. Our children want to know what we believe, how we view life and where our lives are rooted. Invite grandparents to share their childhood memories, their heritage and values with your children. Celebrate the treasure of the spiritual heritage journeying across the previous three or four generations with your children.

EXERCISE 6: Practice Family Hospitality

The home is the first place where our children learn heart values of service and compassion. These values are learned by doing more than by telling. Practice family hospitality through a few of the following approaches.

1. *Event Hospitality*. Preplanned events which welcome guests into the home offer the family time to prepare the home, with training given to each member of the family for their specific tasks. Also, since an event begins and ends on the same day, these short-term approaches to hospitality provide entry-level instruction for children. Event hospitality may be centered around special occasions, but can also be practiced in the ordinary events of your family life.

2. *Overnight Hospitality*. Our home at the beach has become a Bed & Breakfast location for many people, including family, friends, and others. We've taught our kids to help provide linens, beds, towels, food together at table, and conversation and to offer a warm family welcome into the home. Who

has stayed overnight in your home with you this past year? What type of people? How many people? How open is your family to surprises, new challenges, and to stretching your family life, budget and privacy to include others?

3. *Neighborhood Hospitality.* There are many creative ways to reach out into the neighborhood with the warm welcome of love. An important first step is getting to know your neighbors by name. Then, invite them into your home for refreshments. We've taken gifts of food around the neighborhood at Christmas time. We've attended neighborhood "block" parties, sponsored by a neighborhood group, welcoming people to get to know one another informally.

4. *Longer-Term Hospitality.* As mentioned in the chapter above, there are a wide variety of longer-term approaches to hospitality: welcoming into our home an exchange student, a grandparent or grandchildren; offering the gift of adoption or foster care; providing artists or students a place to write, paint or study; offering international students or student interns room and board and a family away from home.

5. *Hospitality Challenge.* Ask yourself the following questions: Who's home do we live in? How can we be more faithful stewards of the lives, possessions, and homes we've been given to dwell in? How can we better serve God through this home, these beds, this furniture, these belongings?

EXERCISE 7: Hospitality Projects That Teach a Lifestyle of Service

There are longer strides a family can make into a lifestyle of hospitality which involve reaching out with open hearts into a very needy world. Try out one of the following this upcoming year.

• Once a year, clear out your closets of unworn clothes and take trips to a local thrift store.

• Child sponsorships: sponsor a needy child in the world through World Vision, Compassion International, or another child sponsorship organization.

• Operation Christmas Child: wrap a shoebox, fill it with gifts according to the guidelines provided by Samaritan's Purse, and mail it to the service center to join with millions of other boxes sent every year to needy children in the world. We've enjoyed participating in this project for many years. For more information, check out *www.samaritanspurse.org*.

• Short-term service projects: Perhaps this is a good year for you to consider taking your children to a needy part of our country or to another country to serve other children and other families.

❧ Chapter Seven ☙

Speak "Friend" and Enter

Doorkeeping
and Spiritual Growth

*Speaking the truth in love, we will in all things grow
up into him who is the Head. . . . From him the whole
body, joined and held together by every supporting
ligament, grows and builds itself up in love, as each
part does its work.* — Ephesians 4:15–16

There is a wonderful scene in J. R. R. Tolkien's story
The Fellowship of the Ring in which Gandalf the wizard
attempts to unlock the stone door into the mountains
of Moria. He tries every secret password that he can
remember. At last he sits down frustrated, as the company anxiously wonders what to do next. Then it hits
him. The message, written in elf runes, simply states,
"Speak, friend, and enter." Gandalf had been trying to
discover the secret password to speak to the door. Then
it came clear how to open the door. "I was wrong after
all," said Gandalf. "The opening word was inscribed on
the archway all the time! The translation should have
been: Say 'Friend' and enter. I had only to speak the

Elvish word for friend and the doors opened. Quite simple."[72] The final approach to spirituality in the family is discovered through doorways of family growth. When families open these doorways, the family will continue to grow, offering friendship to many who come into the life of the family. Without adequate passages and entry points, the family will stifle and growth will be hindered. In chapter seven we will consider several ways to grow into family maturity. These doorways allow the family to come and go, especially when the other six ways into spiritual parenting discussed above are also discovered and put into practice.

Someone Is at the Door

Benedict writes of the task of doorkeeper. *At the door of the monastery, place a sensible person who knows how to take a message and deliver a reply, and whose wisdom keeps him from roaming about* (RB, 66). Family "doorways" include any entrance into the minds and hearts of family members as well as actual doors into the house. These portals might include cell phones, television, and cable.

Every family needs a parent who watches over these doorways. The family doorkeeper decides who to receive and who to turn away. This person also teaches other family members the art of discernment. Here are a few examples.

+ Children need to be taught how and when to answer the phone.

- Teach children what to do when someone's at the front door.

- Besides merely monitoring what our children watch on television, we can teach children how to make wise choices about what they watch.

- We are also wise to offer guidance and "doorkeeping" discernment for our children regarding their choices with music, media, magazines, books, cell phone use and Internet browsing.

More than ever, parents need to be vigilant, watching the digital media "doors" of the family to see who is coming and going.[73] Busy families face many challenges and threats. Some of these come from the outside; some come from within the family. The doorkeeper needs to be stable and wise. When the doorkeeper wanders off, the family is left vulnerable to danger. There will be many inquirers and influences at the family "doors": poor and rich, humble and arrogant, creative and seductive, givers and takers, some who bless and some who curse, some full of sickness and some full of health, the truly needy and con artists, some empty and some overflowing.

The art of discernment enables the doorkeeper to choose when to open doors and when to keep them closed. When the doorkeeper is inattentive, hospitality suffers and people in need might be left waiting outside our doors. The doorkeeper protects the family from distraction and harm. But the doorkeeper also allows for unexpected healthy surprises into the life of the family.

A good doorkeeper listens with discernment, humility, and charity. When a certain "inquirer" is deemed dangerous or harmful to the family, the doorkeeper does not admit such a person or influence. Not all "strangers" are dangerous. Not all "friends" are to be embraced. For example, parents are wise to help kids understand the difference between a stranger and a friend on such social networking computer sites as MySpace and Facebook.

At times, a family's doors need to be locked. We've chosen as a family to "lock out" television from our home. This decision was first made at a family meeting when our children were all in elementary school. Through the years, we regularly revisited this choice, deciding whether or not to connect our lives with the world of television. Over and over, our family has decided against television, opting instead for time out in nature, inside playing games or reading books. When we want to watch a show on television, we go over to other people's homes.

Our family also has a lock-out policy for phone calls during dinner. We ignore any incoming calls, placing higher value upon family meals together than talking on the phone. The only people who get through by phone during mealtimes are family members, and then we invite them to the table by turning on the speaker phone. Our answering machine handles all other calls during mealtime. My wife and I practice this same phone discipline when enjoying time together. With the advent of the cell phone, busy families must be vigilant to ask everyone to turn off cell phones during such times as family meals or family meetings. Within such closed doors, the family can practice true attentiveness and presence with each other.

Parents are wise to follow the guidance of Benedict and place a "sensible person" in the role of family doorkeeper: someone who "knows how to take a message and deliver a reply," and whose wisdom keeps them focused upon the growth of the family. More than merely standing guard or playing policeman, the doorkeeper helps the whole family develop the art of discernment, as well as develop better family communication skills. In this way, your family will continue to mature in your life together.

Facing Difficult Tasks

Not all that happens to us for our good feels good. I recall a monotonous parade of uninteresting jobs during my college summers. I worked on assembly lines, drove vending trucks, delivered pizzas, and bused tables at restaurants. My dad told me these summer jobs were there to teach me what I didn't want to do the rest of my life. Parents know from years of enrollment in the school of hard knocks that character is shaped more by what is difficult than by what is easy. St. James shared this understanding when he wrote, "Consider it pure joy, my brothers, whenever you face trials of many kinds, because you know that the testing of your faith develops perseverance. Perseverance must finish its work so that you may be mature and complete, not lacking anything."[74]

Benedict also addresses the problem of burdensome tasks. Every community has hard work to do and difficult tasks to be accomplished. Rather than avoid this reality, Benedict faces this issue with gentleness and wisdom. He assumes that every member of the monastic family may be assigned tasks that are difficult. He expects monks to accept such assignments with gentleness and obedience. With wise moderation, Benedict allows members of the community to request exemption from certain tasks. A Benedictine family is not a place of slavery or forced labor. The goal is growth and maturity in the love of God. Thus, brothers are given the opportunity to express any gripes to their superior. After the explanation has been made, if the abbot is still determined to hold the monk to the original order, then the brother is asked to accept that this is best. *Trusting God's help, they must in love obey* (RB, 68).

When family members are asked to do a difficult task, parents help them to accept the challenge with a willing spirit. Too often in family life, complaining, grumbling, and disrespect are allowed to take root and grow. Family members then begin to assume that it is the parents' role to give their children a free ride for two decades. At the end of this twenty-year pleasure cruise, parents are expected to deliver mature adults onto the mainland of society. Maturity comes at a price. Some tasks seem impossible at first. If a child feels that a task is beyond their ability, they are free to talk to a parent about it. But children learn to express their concerns with respect. If we see that a child is lazy or unmotivated, we train them appropriately. Regardless of the difficulty of the task assigned, our children are expected to carry out the request to the best of their ability. Arrogant and argumentative children will find their way made even more difficult.

With gentleness and firmness, teach children to walk in the way of respect and mutual love. If parents stick to their decision concerning a difficult task, children will perform the task out of respect for parents, and learn to rely on help. Family spirituality is a training ground for even greater difficulties when we leave home. There are some things in every person's life that must be done, though at first they may appear difficult, painful, or beneath our dignity. God is able to use such tasks to train our lives in patience and love.

Transforming Conflict

Benedict expresses understandable concern for conflict in the monastic family: *If any member assumes any power over those older or, even in regard to the young, flares up and treats them unreasonably, let that one be subjected to the discipline of the Rule* (RB, 70). We are wrong to assume that monasteries are havens of peace and perfection. Every person who enters the abbey brings with them "baggage" from the busy world they've left behind. The monks I know have described the monastic family as a place full of real human beings with very real human struggles. If anything, intentional daily life in the monastic family brings a person's troubles to the surface more readily than in most other lifestyles.

Recognizing the potential within the monastic family for conflict, Benedict provides guidance regarding *the source and occasion for contention* (RB, 69). Conflict and contention in a family may include verbal, emotional, or physical conflict; resisting parental guidance and direction; sibling fights; disrespect; and the unwillingness to forgive one another. Such problems arise in every home.

Every family has its own places of weakness where conflict occurs more frequently. If we want to live with others in peace, we seek to transform conflict by offering gifts of honesty, humility and forgiveness. Peace comes through opening our hearts to one another, admitting our failures, and asking for forgiveness. This is, of course, much easier said than done. The work of waging peace in a family can be like resetting broken bones. Thomas Merton speaks of this in *New Seeds of Contemplation*:

> As long as we are on earth, the love that unites us will bring us suffering by our very contact with one another, because this love is the resetting of a Body of broken bones. Even saints cannot live with saints on this earth without some anguish, without some pain at the differences that come between them.[75]

Bringing the gift of peace may involve the resetting of "broken bones" in your family. Parents who seek to resolve children's fights will encounter their own inner battles and unmet needs. Pain and suffering are an unavoidable part of this way of peace. Over time, those who seek to live in the presence of the Healer of human hearts will experience the wonder of healed relationships. When we are willing to transform conflict in the family, we choose to go through the pain, reach across the dividing wall and offer our hand of friendship. When we trust God to mend our broken lives, we open the door for wholeness to enter our family once again.

Responsibility and Privilege

Privileges are like doorways inviting family members to go out and explore the world. Responsibilities are more like walls, holding up the weight of maturity bearing down upon our lives. The open door of privilege in a family is created by the willingness to carry the load of responsibility. Privilege without responsibility will result in broken lives and a lack of true freedom. Responsibility without privilege is like a home without windows or doors. Maintaining the creative balance between privilege and responsibility demands the best wisdom parents can find.

Responsibility is the ability to respond wisely by putting love into action. As parents, part of our responsibility is to recognize the uniqueness of each child. Each child has unique gifts and burdens to bear. Some burdens come from birth order. A firstborn carries certain firstborn responsibilities. The youngest child has other challenges. With increased responsibility comes increased privilege. With privilege comes responsibility. My wife and I have wrestled together with this tension, regularly seeking wisdom to strike the best balance for each child.

Healthy families have discovered this careful balance between privilege and responsibility. They have doorways of privilege that open out upon the world. Above these openings are hidden weights of responsibilities, the walls that offer protection and stability. As parents, we bear the weight of accountability for all we do. We're responsible for the health and well being of our family. Children are responsible to follow the guidance of their parents. With greater age comes greater responsibility. With greater responsibility comes greater privilege. With greater privilege comes greater maturity.

Age does not naturally produce maturity. Maturity comes through taking responsibility for our own lives and through learning to care for the lives of others. Regardless of age, rank, or privilege, we are responsible to love one another. As Benedict teaches, *No one is to pursue what they judge better for themselves, but instead, what they judge better for someone else. To their fellow monks they show the pure love of brothers and sisters* (RB, 72). In living this truth within the family, we create space for windows and doorways through which flow the sunlight of beauty, friendship, and love.

Leaving Home

There comes a time, according to God's wise plan, when a child grows up and leaves home. Our children are gifts from God. They are entrusted into our care for a short time. Too soon, it seems, they grow up and move on. Most parents with adult children have told me this happens gradually, in fits and starts as our kids find their way in the world. From first pregnancy well into our golden years, we prepare ourselves for the time when our children leave us and when we will leave them. One of the most important tasks for us as parents is to prepare our children to leave home.

Years ago, I officiated at a wedding ceremony in which the mother of the bride was having difficulty letting go of her daughter. Behind the scenes of this beautiful wedding ceremony was a strange landscape of family control. The overbearing parent had refused to respect the choices of her adult children. Her daughter decided to elope without her family's knowledge or blessing. A year and a half later, we were celebrating their married life with a formal wedding ceremony. As I do during every marriage ceremony, I asked for a public declaration by the parents, affirming their support for the bride and groom in their new married life together. Privately, I encouraged the mother of the bride to let her daughter go with her blessing.

At every wedding, there is joy and sadness, gaining and losing. Our children leave us to begin their own families. This is God's design, we remind ourselves, though it doesn't make the grief go away. When we cling to our grown children and refuse to let them go, we cripple their growth into full maturity. When we let our children grow up and leave us, we make room in our hearts and home for their return as mature adults. This too is an essential part of family spirituality.

I believe the best preparation for letting go of our children occurs through daily offering our children to God. As Benedict reminds us, *All absent members should always be remembered at the closing prayer of the work of God* (RB, 67). Every time we offer a prayer for our children, whether they are at home or away, we commit their lives into God's care and ask God to guide them along their way. We let go of our tight grip on our children and allow God to be their guide, whether they are four or forty. In this way we prepare for the hard task of opening the door to their future and letting them leave home.

The Road Is Better Than the End

I tend to look at life as a journey. Cervantes wrote, "The road is better than the end." Each journey has its own ridges and valleys, dry places and springs. All journeys consist of many steps forward and some steps back. Some travel by regret, fear, and apathy. Regret eats away at our hearts with what might have been. Fear erodes the path beneath our feet with what may still be. Apathy quietly seduces us to give up the journey altogether. Some choose to travel by faith, hope, and love. Faith reminds us of the road behind us and of those who walked before us. Hope presses us onward to the destination ahead, presently unseen and unknown. Love unites us, here and now along this road, joining us to God and to one another.

One morning, at the end of a backpacking vacation in Olympic National Park, I asked each family member to choose a stone along the shore of Lake Quinault and name a particular commitment for the new school year that would help us grow in our love for God. After a family prayer of commitment, we cast our stones into the deep blue waters as a visual way to say to God, "We commit our lives to you." God was in our midst, in the heart of our family. We returned home and entered the new school year refreshed and renewed in our faith in God and our love for one another.

Are you hastening toward your heavenly home? asks Benedict. *Then with Christ's help, keep this little rule that we have written for beginners. After that, you can set out for the loftier summits of the teaching and virtues we mentioned above, and under God's protection you will reach them* (RB, 73). So Benedict closes his guidebook for monastic families. As we progress together along the road of family spirituality we can lean upon the principles and practices drawn from Benedict's "little rule that we have written for beginners." Family spirituality is available for busy families but it does not happen in a hurry. Like the trails we've hiked summer after summer as a family into the high meadowlands of the Olympics, the way into family spirituality unfolds gradually, step by step as we faithfully keep along the path. Life in the family is intended to lead us closer to God. Let nothing become more important than the love of God. With God's help, I hope this family guidebook may assist you and your family along the way in your journey together.

FAMILY GROWTH EXERCISES

EXERCISE 1: Top Ten Family Media Habits

These media habits are adapted from James P. Steyer, *The Other Parent* (New York: Atria Books, 2002). Choose a few of these to employ in your home this month.

1. *Establish good media habits early*. On average, children watch 44 hours of television per week. Children spend more time consuming media than going to school or spending time with family. Children spend more time consuming media than being involved with creative play or physical exercise. How much media are your children consuming daily?

2. *No TV or computer in a child's room*. Two-thirds of all children over age 8 in this country have a television in their bedroom. One-third of children ages 2 to 7 also have a television in their bedroom. Agree as a family where televisions and computers will be located in your home. Make media a family event, not a private act. Be proactive and place all televisions and computers in common areas such as family rooms. I believe children are better off without televisions in their bedrooms.

3. *Set a media diet and stick to it*. See digital media as food for the mind and heart. Ask yourself, what food is being served to my children? Create a media diet for your family. Keep a media diet journal or family media log for a few weeks. Assess your media diet. Set better limits and balances to

your current consumption. Work these things out together in family meetings, setting limits, making media choices together.

4. *Teach a child to ask permission to use media.* Make media use "by appointment." Allow no presumed right to unlimited media consumption in the home. Media use is a privilege not a requirement or right. Make media a choice not a habit.

5. *Watch and listen with your kids.* Interact with your children in their media environment. Speyer describes adults as tourists in a foreign land, with children as the natives of media-land, familiar with the culture and language of media. Sit, watch, listen and play with your children in their media world. Join children in their TV shows, their video games, their music. Tell them what you like and dislike about their choices. Share your values, your beliefs and your views with your children.

6. *Set clear rules about your child's media use in other homes.* Let other parents know about your children's media limits. As a family, work out together your media use guidelines before sending children to sleep-overs. Address the issue head-on, positively, proactively, rather than covertly, negatively or reactively.

7. *Ask your pediatrician to review your child's media use at an annual checkup.* The American Academy of Pediatrics (AAP) recommends that pediatricians should review media consumption as part of

children's annual physical exams. Pediatricians are increasingly raising concerns about media's impact on children, seeing media as a public health issue (violence, sexuality, obesity, cardiology). At your child's next annual check-up, ask your pediatrician to talk with your children about their media consumption, as well as basic nutritional, diet assessment.

8. *Teach media literacy.* Learn how to think critically about the media. Teach children to think critically about media. Develop media literacy, the "ability to access, analyze, evaluate, process media."

9. *Share positive media experiences.* Spend quality time with children enjoying positive media time. Plan, choose and set up family events for good media experiences. Use digital media to teach children values, build knowledge and unite the family together.

10. *Switch media machines "OFF."* Get more comfortable turning media off in your home. Instead, read to your child, go outside for a walk in a park, or do an art project together.

EXERCISE 2: Family Nature Walk

Doorways in the home are to welcome people into the family, but also to get family members together outside. One of our favorite family activities over the years has been taking family nature walks. Below I offer a simple guide for taking children into the wonder of God's creation.

Step One: Plan a family nature walk. Set aside some time one day during this month to take a nature walk as a family. Check out the possible hiking trails in your area, including those within a short drive. Commit a set time during the day to meet together for this family activity.

Step Two: Prepare for the nature walk. Pack a daypack with necessary items for the nature walk, including water bottles, snacks, collection bags, journals. Decide on footwear and clothing. Bring along a digital camera if possible.

Step Three: Take a walk together. While on the walk, ask every family member to observe specific aspects of God's creation, using eyes, ears, noses, and hands to gather information about nature. One family member may want to specialize in stones and rocks (geology); another in trees and leaves (botany); another in animal life (zoology); another in weather patterns (meteorology). Write down observations in a journal. Collect samples if appropriate. Take photos of various aspects of nature.

Step Four: Share the walk. After returning from the nature walk, sit together as a family and show and tell what you've learned and discovered. Show photos taken during the walk. We have stones, feathers, seashells and other objects of nature on nearly every window sill and shelf in our home from hundreds of nature walks taken together as a family over the years. They offer our family reminders to the many beautiful memories we've shared together in God's wildlife sanctuary of nature.

EXERCISE 3: Family Media Survey

How much media do we consume every day? At a family meeting, ask family members to share their views and preferences.

Television

+ Favorite TV channel:

+ Favorite TV show:

+ # of hours per day TV is on (national average is 6 hours per day):

Computer

+ Favorite computer game:

+ # of hours per day computer is used in your home (including Internet, e-mailing, gaming):

+ Location of computers in our home:

+ How many "friends" does each family member have on their computer social network page (such as MySpace or Facebook)? How many of these "friends" have been introduced to the rest of the family?

Video/DVD

+ Favorite video game or movie rental:

+ Type of video game system(s) in our home:

+ How often do parents sit with kids to play video games?

+ # of hours per day on video games/movies (on average)

- What types of games are inappropriate or unhealthy for our family?

Radio/CD/MP3 Player

- Favorite types of music:

- # of hours per day radio/CD player/MP3 player is playing:

- What types of music are inappropriate or unhealthy for our family?

Cell phone

- How many cell phones are in use in our family?

- How many cell phone calls per day does each family member make?

- How many times per day are cell phones used for instant messaging or texting?

EXERCISE 4: Writing a Family "Rule of Life"

The following exercise may be used by the whole family when children are old enough to participate in this type of activity, or by parents when children are still very young. The intent is to better understand the core values, principles and practices of your life as a family. Just as businesses and non-profit groups often write a "mission statement" to describe their purpose, this exercise invites families to better define and clarify their family purpose by writing a family *regula* or "rule of life." Here are a few steps in the process:

1. *Study together*

- Buy a family journal — an empty book or spiral notebook.

- Collect wisdom sayings, helpful teachings and good advice concerning parenting, love, and family life.

- Research books on your shelves or in your local library or bookstore for the best ideas from novels, poems, non-fiction, and biographies giving guidance for your family life. Review the best wisdom from the Bible concerning family life and love. Write these ideas into the family journal.

2. *Discuss family values, goals, and purposes*

- Gather together for a family meeting.

- Ask everyone to write down five words or sentences (depending on their age) that best describe the best way for family to live together. Ask family members, "What do you think is our family mission, goal or purpose?"

- Discuss these family values and perspectives, offering no critiques or negative input, but having a "scribe" write down these ideas in the family journal.

- Ask wise people to give you their definition of "family" and add these statements into your journal.

3. *Write a first draft of a family "Rule of Life"*

- Gather the family for another family meeting.

- Ask everyone to help write your family "Rule of Life."

- Have a white board and dry-erase markers, or large newsprint to write out a first draft of your family "Rule of Life."

- Include in your family "Rule of Life" some of the following items: the purpose of your family, core family values, commitments and spiritual practices.

4. Adopt your family "Rule of Life"

- Read the completed family "Rule of Life" aloud to the family.

- Offer a family prayer asking for God's support to enable you to live more fully according to your family "Rule of Life."

- Review the family "Rule of Life" at least annually as a family.

EXERCISE 5: Support in Finding Parental Balance

There are many ways to get out of balance as parents. Mark the statement in each category that best represents your approach to parenting.

1. Attention
   - ___ We spoil our child with too much extra attention.
   - ___ We do not spend enough quality time with our child.

2. Responsibilities
   - ___ We make our child carry too heavy a load.
   - ___ We expect very little from our child around the house.

3. Conflict Resolution

____ We rely on our child to settle family fights.

____ We seldom bring the family together to solve conflicts in the home.

4. Listening

____ We ignore a child who is speaking to us.

____ We tend to bend over backwards to listen to our children.

5. Work

____ We've neglected the family for the sake of a career.

____ We've often neglected our work for the sake of our kids.

6. Favoritism

____ We play favorites, giving special attention to one child at the expense of another.

____ We've gone overboard trying to treat each child exactly the same.

7. Respect

____ We tolerate a fair amount of disrespect in our family.

____ We demand that children be respectful of others.

8. Accountability

____ We refuse to hold a child accountable for his actions.

____ We are probably a bit excessive in holding our children accountable for their actions.

9. Expectations

___ We expect our children to grow up quickly and act like adults.

___ We have expected too little from our children and even hindered them from maturing.

10. Support

___ We allow kids to wallow in their messes and problems.

___ We've sought wise support (both personal and professional) for our children in their problems.

EXERCISE 6: "Just a Spoonful of Sugar" and Other Wisdom for Parents

In the classic Disney film *Mary Poppins,* Jane and Michael Banks write up a list describing their ideal nanny — cheery disposition, wit, kindness, etc. After singing their wishes to their father, Mr. Banks gets angry, tears up the list and throws it into the fire. Magically, Mary Poppins arrives, bringing the children's list intact. She brings not just "a spoonful of sugar to help the medicine go down," but also her "no nonsense" approach to raising children. In this exercise, name some of your ideals for parenting. Bring to mind the wisdom sayings, Bible passages, proverbs, and helpful guidance you've received from your children, parents, grandparents or other sources. Also, review the previous chapters, and write down those qualities that you hope to see grow in the heart of your home.

Wisdom for raising children

♦ Wisdom you've gained from your children:

♦ Wisdom from the Bible, including instructions, promises, proverbs or truths:

♦ Wisdom from parents, grandparents and other people you've met:

♦ Wisdom from the heart:

♦ Wisdom from books you've read:

♦ Helpful ideas found in *The Busy Family's Guide to Spirituality:*

♦ Wisdom from other sources:

EXERCISE 7: Hiking Tips for Families

I've often referred to our family hiking adventures in these pages and view family spirituality as a lifelong journey. In this final family exercise, I offer a few practical ideas for going out on family backpacking adventures. Enjoy a family hike this season, exploring the beauty and bounty of nature.

1. *Start with day hikes and build up to longer adventures.* Begin "hiking" around the neighborhood, in a local park or in an area arboretum. Plan hikes according to the ages of your children. We spent years taking short day hikes within an hour's drive of our home. Year after year, we gradually built up to longer hiking adventures as our children grew. Involve your children in the planning process.

2. *Study maps and trail guidebooks.* Go to your local library or bookstore to study maps and trail guidebooks featuring hiking trails in your area. We've purchased hiking books written especially for families. Look for books that offer detailed information for trails in your region. We study topographical maps and backpackers trail guidebooks in preparation for our annual family backpacking trips.

3. *Decide upon times and places.* Consider the time of year, weather, and trail conditions, as well as time of day for your hike. Plan your hike according to the ability of your youngest hiker with the goal that everyone comes home looking forward to the next family hike. Some trails are loop hikes. Some require dropping a second car at the other end of the trail. Some hikes will take you "up and back" along the same trail.

4. *Gear up.* Over the years, keep adding to your hiking gear, growing into this family activity gradually. At first, you'll need a day-pack, ten-essentials, close-toed hiking shoes, and water bottles. Check out hiking outfitter companies such as REI (*www.rei.com*). REI features "expert advice" on their website including excellent gear lists for day hikes, backpacking and other outdoor adventures.

5. *Train and prepare.* Success on the trail starts at home. Training includes physical fitness before stepping out at a trailhead. Prepare with basic

physical exercise weeks before attempting any strenuous family hiking adventure. Preparations also include gathering supplies, food, equipment and letting others know where you are going. Establish basic safety guidelines and ground rules with the family before heading out.

6. *Heading out from the trailhead.* As you lock up your car at a trailhead, be sure to take all valuables with you. Double-check each family member for appropriate clothing, footwear, hats, and gear. Always carry the "ten-essentials" when hiking. For lists of these essentials go to *www.rei.com* or *www.mountaineers.org.* We always offer a short prayer of thanks at the trailhead before starting out on our family hiking adventure.

7. *Enjoying family adventures.* The real goal is not "getting there" but enjoying the adventure along the way. We love to stop along the way to notice wildlife and wildflowers, take photos, enjoy snack breaks, or take off our boots and soak our feet in a mountain stream. As John Muir once wrote, "Everybody needs beauty as well as bread, places to play in and pray in where nature may heal and cheer and give strength to the body and soul."

❦ Epilogue ❧

Parenting
Is for Beginners

The reason we have written this guidebook is that, by observing it in families, we can show that we have some degree of virtue and the beginnings of family spiritual life. [76]
— *The Rule of St. Benedict,* chap. 73

Family spirituality is a peculiar way of life. Just as we begin to figure it out, our children head off to kindergarten or enter adolescence and the rules seem to change. By the time we've become veterans at child-raising, our kids have the audacity to leave us. When this book was first published in 2000, our sons were all in their teen years, still living at home, with two in high school and one in middle school. In the past ten years, our sons have all left home, leaving us with an "empty nest." The first few years after our youngest son left for college, my wife and I felt a quiet sense of loss. We still miss being with our kids on a daily basis.

When our children depart into their adult lives, walking their own paths, parents can experience a strange

215

mix of feelings including regret and relief, satisfaction and emptiness. My wife and I have taken delight over the years in the sound of our sons' voices, their hugs, their playfulness, and our prayers together. In the place of the sound of children playing, a quiet has come over our home. Like a fountain spring at the center of a garden, God fills this quiet garden with refreshment, goodness and love. In the presence of God, we find the inner comfort and guidance to watch our kids from afar and wait to see how their adult years unfold. As John Milton once wrote, "they also serve who only stand and wait."

In the quiet garden time of life, parents with grown children find themselves reflecting upon their years of raising children. Soul-searching questions arise in our hearts. Did we adequately prepare them for adulthood? What could we have done better? We revisit the past in our memories, sometimes recalling our failures and shortcomings as parents. Dr. Mark Gundy, Ph.D., a family therapist, writes, "This phase in a [parent's] life can create feelings of loss and make it important to go through a time of grieving."[77]

The journey of daily parenting children in the home lasts a brief time, only two or three decades. When our first child is born, the parenting journey ahead seems to go on and on, without any clear sense of a final destination. For new parents, college graduation is the last thing on their mind. Rather, parents of infants wonder when and if their child will ever begin sleeping through the night. Looking back down the trail as parents of three sons in their twenties, we have found ourselves savoring the memories, cherishing sweet moments we shared together over the years, and enjoying the company of our kids as adults, grateful for the generous gift of family life.

Since 2000, two of our sons have married, bringing two beautiful daughters-in-love into our family. Along with the empty nest comes an expanding family as we welcome our sons' wives and their families into our heart and home. We look forward to the time in the future when we will become grandparents, knowing that grandchildren and great-grandchildren will open up whole new chapters in our family journal.

Another significant change in my life since the first writing of this book was becoming a Benedictine Oblate in January, 2006 at Mount Angel Benedictine Abbey. This lifelong promise calls me daily to live according to the way of St. Benedict and the basic spiritual principles found in *The Rule of St. Benedict*. The further I walk along this path, the more Benedict has proven, in my day-to-day life, to be a reliable guide.

As parents, we need wise guidance to face the challenges of family life. Some problems are unique to 21st-century families. Most are the same difficulties parents have faced for centuries. Families change. Communities change. Cultures change. Societies change. But human nature remains largely the same. Children still cry out to be loved. Parents still cry out for support in the challenge of parenting. Some adults find themselves parenting alone without the support of a spouse or partner. Others find their spouse doesn't share their faith convictions regarding parenting and they press on, alone in the spiritual endeavor of raising children.

Older folks who thought their parenting days were over find themselves in their retirement years actively raising their grandchildren because of difficulties their adult children have encountered. Within all these challenges, God continues to invite parents to train a child "in the way she should go," that is, in the way of love.

Although we have been parenting for nearly three decades, we still feel like novices as we journey into the country of family spirituality. Fortunately, parenting is for beginners. Children are mysteries a lifetime will not completely unveil. There are no degrees, no certificates, and little training for new parents, except the practical experience of raising children. Often in our day, teens have children before they have reached adulthood. This is not as bad as it might seem at first, as long as those teens have a supportive group of adults around them. Teens are excellent learners. Parents who accept themselves as amateurs also make good learners. At the root of the word "amateur" is the Latin word for love. Amateurs are those who do what they do for the sake of love. This little book, a guide for family spirituality, is written for beginners and amateurs in the love life called parenting.

I have based much of this book upon the belief that what Benedict discovered and taught to his monastic family fifteen hundred years ago remains true today. At the heart of Benedict's communal vision is *life-together* spirituality, a family seeking to put love in action with God as our guide. I believe God is inviting a whole new generation of parents to seek support in their family journey "further up and further in," to borrow a phrase from C. S. Lewis's book, *The Last Battle,* from the *Chronicles of Narnia* series of children's books. As one of the characters in Lewis's book declares, "I have come home at last! This is my real country! I belong here. This is the land I have been looking for all my life, though I never knew it till now. Come further up, come further in!"[78]

Many busy parents in the twenty-first century are looking for an approach to parenting which feels like a place where they can "come home at last," a style of parenting where they feel they truly belong. Into this new country of parenting, we journey with our children, seeking out fellow travelers who call to us to "come further up, come further in!" We hope the path we follow will lead us to the land we have been looking for all our lives, though we "never knew it till now."

Old paths intrigue me. When I come upon an old trail, I look as far as I can, wondering who made the path, whose feet have walked upon that way, and where it will lead. We are wise to look long and hard at the old paths, including the ancient paths of family spirituality. When Benedict looked at his world in the early sixth century, he saw busyness, corruption, and instability. The path he chose turned away from the ills of society, climbed up a mountain, through a garden gate, into family spiritual life together with others. Upon that mountain, surrounded by a community of fellow travelers and pilgrims, Benedict wrote a guidebook for their spiritual life together.

As we journey into this new millennium, millions are wondering where the twenty-first century will lead us.

If we are focused enough to stand still and look, we will see Benedict's way marked clearly on the best maps. If we are wise enough to ask where the good path leads, we will hear an old saint's voice calling us to follow this way. If we are courageous enough to walk in the wisdom of Benedict, we will find our children and grandchildren growing in goodness, wisdom, and love. As parents, when we commit to journeying with our children into family spirituality, we will indeed find rest, renewal, and refreshment for our soul, for our family, and for our world.

Acknowledgments

I am grateful for the community of people encircling our lives. Thanks to our parents, Don and Berta Robinson, Sigrid Hudson, and the late Bill Hudson, and to our families for their love and support in the adventure of parenting. Gwendolin Herder and Sylke Jackson of the Crossroad Publishing Company graced this work with their editorial guidance. Several monks, including Father Tim Clark of Seattle; Brother Martin of Our Lady of Guadalupe, Oregon; Brother John Albert formerly of Monastery of the Holy Spirit, Georgia; and Father Pius X Harding, Oblate Director at Mount Angel Benedictine Abbey, Oregon, have offered insight into the Benedictine way of life. More importantly, they've offered friendship and spiritual direction to me and countless others seeking guidance in Benedictine spirituality. Thanks to Valerie Ryan, owner of Cannon Beach Book Company, Cannon Beach, Oregon, for her editorial critiques to improve this book. I'm also grateful for the support of our many friends and wise mentors. We have not raised our children alone. The people of Community Presbyterian Church, Cannon Beach, have been our family of faith since 1993. Many other parents and community members, including coaches, teachers, neighbors and employers have also helped us raise our kids in wisdom and love. We owe a debt of gratitude to many family friends including Jon and Doreen Broderick, Ben and Judy Herr, Doug and Laurie Dougherty, Margo Lalich and Michael Burger, Karin Schulz, Jay and Laura Stewart, and John Boril among others, who have built up our lives with their love and helped raise our children. Finally, I am grateful to the members of my family, including Trina, my best friend and wife, our three grown sons and two daughters-in-love, including Jonathan and Christina, Stefan and Jessica, and Thomas.

Notes

1. In general, chapter 1 (Blueprints) covers chapters 1–7 of the *Rule;* chapter 2 (Spirituality) covers chapters 8–20 of the *Rule;* chapter 3 (Training) covers chapters 21–30 of the *Rule;* chapter 4 (Health) covers chapters 31–41 of the *Rule;* chapter 5 (Life Together) covers chapters 42–52 of the *Rule;* chapter 6 (Hospitality) covers chapters 53–65 of the *Rule;* and chapter 7 (Growth) covers chapters 66–73 of the *Rule.*

2. All quotations from *The Rule of St. Benedict* are italicized throughout the text. Citations from the *Rule* are taken from *The Rule of St. Benedict* (Collegeville, MN: Liturgical Press, 1982) and are used with the permission of Liturgical Press. The citations have been modified here in the interests of inclusive language. For a helpful resource to better understand Benedict's *Rule,* I recommend Joan Chittister, O.S.B., *The Rule of Benedict: Insights for the Ages* (New York: Crossroad, 1995), 191.

3. Francis Hodgson Burnett, *The Secret Garden* (New York: Grosset & Dunlap, 1998), 77, 79.

4. Jeremiah 6:16.

5. Dorothy Corkille Briggs, *Your Child's Self-Esteem* (New York: Doubleday, 1975), 312.

6. In Latin, *Ora et labora.*

7. Proverbs 10:19.

8. Elaine St. James, *Simplify Your Life: 100 Ways to Make Family Life Easier and More Fun* (Kansas City, MO: Andrews McMeel Publishing, 1997).

9. James 3:10–11.

10. Mother Teresa, *Love: Always a Fruit in Season* (Fort Collins, CO: Ignatius Press, 1987), 129.

11. Psalm 67:1.

12. Galatians 5:22–23.

13. Deuteronomy 6:5–9.

14. Luke 11:1.

15. Dietrich Bonhoeffer, *Psalms: The Prayer Book of the Bible* (Minneapolis: Augsburg Publishing House, 1970), 64.

16. Here are a few family music resources which you may find helpful for singing together in the home or in the car. *Wee Sing Songbooks* (Price Stern Sloan, 2005), compiled by Pamela Conn Beall and Susan Hagen Nipp. The *Wee Sing* series of eight family songbooks are directed towards children ages 4–8, including such titles as *Wee Sing Bible Songs, Wee Sing for Christmas, Wee Sing Children's Songs and Fingerplays, Wee Sing Silly Songs.* Look up Peter Blood and Annie Patterson, eds., *Rise Up Singing: The Group Singing Songbook* (Sing Out Publications, 2004), with foreword by Pete Seeger. Recently, our family has begun to sing Taizé songs written by the Taizé Community in France. See *Songs & Prayers from Taizé* (GIA Publications, Inc., 1991). Also, check out the Taizé website for samples of these songs, at *www.taize.fr/en.* For an excellent sing-along songbook for older children and youth including a wide variety of types of songs, see *Songs* (Songs and Creations, 2008) by Yohann Anderson. This collection features 1,150 songs for every occasion.

17. See Exodus 20:1–17 and Deuteronomy 5:6–21.

18. Exodus 20:8, 11.

19. Deuteronomy 5:12.

20. Advent is Latin for "coming."

21. This craft is best for children who are old enough to work with candles, hot wax and eggs. For more information on how to begin decorating Ukrainian Easter Eggs in your home, go to the Ukrainian online gift shop at *www.ukrainiangiftshop.com* or pick up *Luba's Ukrainian Easter Egg Decorating Kit.*

22. Gertrud Mueller Nelson, *To Dance with God: Family Ritual and Community Celebration* (Mahwah, NJ: Paulist Press, 1986), 45.

23. Psalm 78:4.

24. Brother Lawrence, *The Practice of the Presence of God* (New Kensington, PA: Whitaker House, 1982), 33–34.

25. Mark 1:35.

26. Colossians 3:12.

27. Simon Weil, quoted from *On Earth as It Is in Heaven* (New York: Penguin Books, 1994), 3.

28. Brother Lawrence, *The Practice of the Presence of God,* 33.

29. Ephesians 6:4.

30. Hebrews 12:11.

31. Hebrews 10:25.

32. Quoted from *www.top-basketball-coaching.com/April_2007 _Wooden_Wisdoms.htm,* March 17, 2009.

33. Matthew 13:52.

34. James 2:13.

35. Hebrews 4:12.

36. Hebrews 4:14–16.

37. Sarah McElwain, *Saying Grace: Blessings for the Family Table* (San Francisco: Chronicle Books LLC, 2003), 6.

38. See Luke 24:13–35.

39. Luke 24:35.

40. Acts 4:32.

41. Mother Teresa, *A Gift for God* (New York: Harper & Row, 1975), 11–12.

42. Isaiah 58:10–11.

43. 2 Corinthians 1:3–4.

44. Proverbs 17:1.

45. See *www.casacolumbia.org/Absolutenm/articlefiles/Family_ Dinners_9_03_03.pdf.*

For other similar studies, look into *www.familyfirst.org.nz/index .cfm/Eating_together.*

46. Isaiah 58:6–7.

47. I've adapted this phrase from Psalm 4:8. "I will lie down and sleep in peace, for you alone, O LORD, make me dwell in safety." Following guidance from the *Rule,* three night-time Psalms are sung for memory every night during Compline in Benedictine monasteries around the world, including Psalms 4, 91, and 134. We have spoken Psalm 4:8 as a night-time blessing in our home for years.

48. "As a photographer," states Thomas Robinson, "I strive to glorify God by sharing God's splendor in creation. Photography is a visual form of communication that reveals the glory of God in a scene. My passion in nature and landscape photography is rooted in my faith and my love for the deeper glory found in every

corner of creation." See *http://gallery.ecola.us/* to view Thomas's online nature photography galleries.

49. Dr. Jeff Sigafoos, 1999, *www.centerforcreativeplay.org.*

50. C. S. Lewis, *The Screwtape Letters* (New York: Macmillan, 1961), 49–52.

51. For more ideas on incorporating creativity and playfulness in your parenting look into Lawrence Cohen's *Playful Parenting* (New York: Ballantine Books, 2001).

52. Psalm 139:9–10.

53. Genesis 31:49.

54. Numbers 6:24–26.

55. Psalm 121:7.

56. Psalm 91:1.

57. Isaiah 12:3.

58. Richard Louv, *Last Child in the Woods: Saving our Children from Nature-Deficit Disorder* (New York: Workman Publishing Company, 2005).

59. For two excellent books of home science experiments for children ages 9–12, both by Tom Robinson, see *The Everything Kids' Science Experiments Book: Boil Ice, Float Water, Measure Gravity — Challenge the World Around You!* (Adams Media, 2001); and *Everything Kids' Magical Science Experiments Book: Dazzle Your Friends and Family by Making Magical Things Happen!* (Adams Media, 2007). These best-selling books are written by my youngest brother, a high school science teacher and a wonderful father of two great kids.

60. 1 Peter 4:9.

61. James 1:27.

62. Leo Tolstoy, *What Men Live By* (New York: Peter Pauper Press), 57–58.

63. The nation's oldest and largest mentoring organization, *Big Brothers Big Sisters of America,* has had more than a century of experience of offering adult-child mentoring, with the safety of the child their most important concern. Mentoring a child requires the gift of time and a willingness to share our lives with others. For more information, see their website at *www.bbbs.org.*

64. Luke 2:19.

65. These ten portraits are taken from the following passages of the New Testament: Luke 1:26–38; 1:39–45; 2:1–20; Matthew 2:13–15; Luke 2:41–52; John 2:1–11; Mark 3:20–21, 31–34; John 19:25–27; Luke 24:1–8; Acts 1:14.

66. Luke 1:46–47 (New International Readers Version).

67. As Psalm 150:6 declares, "Let everything that has breath praise the Lord. Alleluia!"

68. Dorothy Law Nolte, *Children Learn What They Live* (New York: Workman, 1998), 107.

69. Ibid.

70. Proverbs 24:3–4.

71. Luke 2:19.

72. J. R. R. Tolkien, *The Fellowship of the Ring* (New York: Ballantine Books, 1954), 401–2.

73. For a parent-friendly resource which contains reviews and evaluations of digital media, including movies, television, games, websites and music, look into *www.commonsensemedia.org,* founded by James P. Speyer, author of *The Other Parent: The Inside Story of the Media's Effect on Our Children* (New York: Atria Books, 2002).

74. James 1:2–4.

75. Thomas Merton, *New Seeds of Contemplation* (New York: New Directions Publishing, 1961), 72.

76. I've slightly adapted this sentence from the final chapter of the *Rule,* to speak directly to parents and families.

77. Quoted from "Portland Family," August 2008, 10, in an article written by Mary O. Parker.

78. C. S. Lewis, *The Last Battle* (New York: Macmillan Publishing Co., Inc., 1956), 162.

Of Related Interest

Tian Dayton, Ph.D.
MODERN MOTHERING
How to Teach Kids to Say What They Feel
and Feel What They Say

From her appearances on *Oprah* to her role as a mother, professor, and counselor, Tian Dayton helps us to see the importance of the mother-child relationship. How do children actually learn to articulate their emotional needs? Dr. Dayton offers a remarkable solution, showing how mothers can guide their children to emotional literacy in order to find their true selves, express creativity, and lead productive lives.

0-8245-2340-7, paperback

Of Related Interest

Thomas Keating
THE HEART OF THE WORLD
An Introduction to Contemplative Christianity

The Christian heritage is rich in contemplative wisdom literature and practices. As fresh and vibrant today as when it was first published, this classic is essential to a deeper understanding of the spiritual center of Christianity.

It is especially written for those who, while benefiting from a spiritual practice in one of the other world religions, want to preserve or renew their fundamental commitment to Christianity.

978-0-8245-2495-1, paperback

Of Related Interest

Donna-Marie Cooper O'Boyle
THE HEART OF MOTHERHOOD
Finding Holiness in the Catholic Home

When dirty dishes and laundry pile up, it's easy to believe that the call to sanctity is for someone else. But this inspiring book written by a Catholic mother of five and based on the teachings of Mother Teresa shows us how faith can support mothers in their most holy task — raising children.

978-0-8245-2403-6, paperback

Of Related Interest

Joan Chittister
THE RULE OF BENEDICT
Insights for the Ages

The Benedictine way, the author contends, "is the spirituality of the twenty-first century because it deals with issues facing us now — stewardship, relationships, authority, community, balance, work, simplicity, prayer, and spiritual and psychological development."

0-8245-2503-5, paperback